Born

CATHY FREEMAN
My Story

HI GUYS,

I hope you enjoy my story, and that it inspires you to chase after your dreams, too!

♡ Cathy

Puffin Books

Born to Run

CATHY FREEMAN
My Story

Puffin Books

PUFFIN BOOKS

Published by the Penguin Group
Penguin Group (Australia)
250 Camberwell Road
Camberwell, Victoria 3124, Australia
(a division of Pearson Australia Group Pty Ltd)
Penguin Group (USA) Inc.
375 Hudson Street, New York, New York 10014, USA
Penguin Group (Canada)
90 Eglinton Avenue East, Suite 700,
Toronto ON M4P 2Y3, Canada
(a division of Pearson Penguin Canada Inc.)
Penguin Books Ltd
80 Strand, London WC2R ORL, England
Penguin Ireland
25 St Stephen's Green, Dublin 2, Ireland
(a division of Penguin Books Ltd)
Penguin Books India Pvt Ltd
11, Community Centre, Panchsheel Park, New Delhi -110 017, India
Penguin Group (NZ)
67 Apollo Drive, Mairangi Bay, Auckland 1310, New Zealand
(a division of Pearson New Zealand Ltd)
Penguin Books (South Africa) (Pty) Ltd
24 Sturdee Avenue, Rosebank, Johannesburg 2196, South Africa

Penguin Books Ltd, Registered Offices: 80 Strand, London WC2R ORL, England

First published by Penguin Group (Australia), a division of Pearson Australia Group Pty Ltd, 2007

1 3 5 7 9 10 8 6 4 2

Text copyright © Catherine Freeman Enterprises Pty Limited, 2007

The moral right of the author has been asserted.

All rights reserved. Without limiting the rights under copyright reserved above, no part of this publication may be reproduced, stored in or introduced into a retrieval system, or transmitted, in any form or by any means (electronic, mechanical, photocopying, recording or otherwise), without the prior written permission of both the copyright owner and the above publisher of this book.

Text and cover design by Elissa Christian © Penguin Group (Australia)
Front cover photograph by Scott Barbour/Allsport
Back cover photograph by Nick Wilson/Allsport
Typeset in 12/19 pt Fairfield Light by Palmer Higgs, Box Hill, Victoria
Printed in Australia by McPherson's Printing Group, Maryborough, Victoria

National Library of Australia
Cataloguing-in-Publication data:

Freeman, Cathy, 1973– .
Born to run: my story.

ISBN-13: 978 0 14 330238 4.
ISBN-10: 0 14 330238 8.

1. Freeman, Cathy, 1973– . 2. Women athletes, Aboriginal Australian – Biography.
3. Athletes, Aboriginal Australian – Biography. 4. Women athletes – Australia – Biography.
5. Runners (Sports) – Australia – Biography. I. Title.

796.42092

www.puffin.com.au

To my parents,
Bruce and Cecelia Barber,
for teaching me self-love,
power and freedom

Contents

MY STORY		ix
CHAPTER 1	Running Free	1
CHAPTER 2	My Family + Me	13
CHAPTER 3	New Dad	23
CHAPTER 4	World's Greatest Athlete	31
CHAPTER 5	School Days	41
CHAPTER 6	Bright Future	55
CHAPTER 7	Running for Australia	63
CHAPTER 8	First Olympics	73

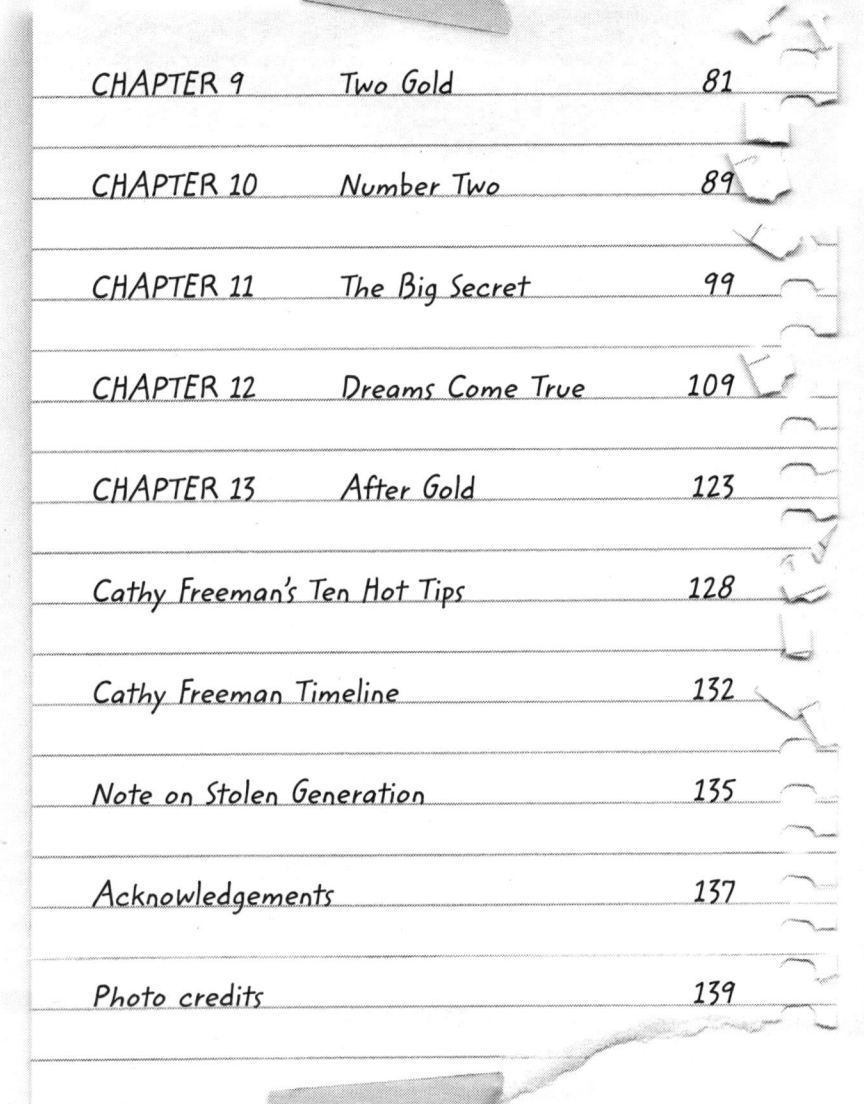

CHAPTER 9	Two Gold	81
CHAPTER 10	Number Two	89
CHAPTER 11	The Big Secret	99
CHAPTER 12	Dreams Come True	109
CHAPTER 13	After Gold	123
Cathy Freeman's Ten Hot Tips		128
Cathy Freeman Timeline		132
Note on Stolen Generation		135
Acknowledgements		137
Photo credits		139

My Story

My mother once told me a story about the time before I was born. She told me that her spiritual mother, Muriel, came to bless me while I was still inside her belly. As I lay peacefully in the womb, Muriel put her hands on Mum's stomach and spoke out loud. She prayed that I would be a 'fortunate one'.

It's amazing to hear Mum tell that story now, because when I think about my life, I have been very fortunate. I've got a great family and lots of good friends. I've travelled all over the world competing for Australia, and at the age of twenty-seven I even won a gold medal at the Olympics.

Sometimes I still wonder how it happened. When I was growing up, I didn't feel that different to anyone else – I was just a little Aboriginal girl who could run fast. But I've learnt that anyone, no matter who they are, can make the most of what they have. I was born with a good body for running, but I also had a dream – the dream to be the very best I could be. For me, running made that dream come true.

CHAPTER 1
Running Free

My first ever race could have been a complete disaster. I was eight and it was athletics day at St Joseph's Primary School. I had to represent Gold House in the 80m sprint, but I almost missed it because I was hiding in the toilets.

'Catherine! Where are you? Your race is on NOW!'

I could hear my sports teacher, Mrs Bauldry,

looking for me. I was supposed to be at the starting line with the other kids, but stage fright had set in. I was feeling shy because a few of the parents had turned up to watch us.

Eventually Mrs Bauldry managed to coax me out of the bathroom. 'Quickly,' she said. 'Hurry or you'll miss it!'

I rushed towards the oval where the races were being held. I was in such a hurry, I didn't look where I was going and ran straight into a wire fence.

Ouch! A piece of wire had poked me in the eye. It was stinging, but I knew I didn't have time to do anything about it. I ran the rest of the way to the oval and made it to the starting line just in time.

'On your marks... get set... go!' yelled one of the teachers.

I took off, pumping my legs as fast as I could. My eye was still hurting so I kept it tightly closed and ran with only one eye open. I'm not sure how I managed to stay in my lane and not bump into the other kids who were running.

It was my first race so I wasn't expecting much – I just ran. And somehow I ended up winning!

It didn't take me long to realise that running was something I was good at. Later that year, Mrs Bauldry entered me in the state primary school titles. The titles were held in Brisbane and we were all billeted with different families. Mrs Bauldry had given me a new shirt to wear and also a pair of blue running shoes with spikes. I'd never owned spikes before so I didn't know you weren't supposed to wear them in the house. I'll never forget the look on my host mother's face when I walked down the hall, ripping out bits of her carpet along the way.

'Whoa!' she said. 'Catherine, love, don't you think it might be a good idea to take those off while you're inside?'

I heard a big tearing sound as I lifted my foot one more time and realised what I'd been doing. 'Um, sure,' I said.

I won my first gold medal at those titles and when I got home Mum was waiting for me on the front porch. When she found out I'd won she smothered me with hugs and kisses.

'Ohh, Catherina, I'm so proud of you.' she said. 'So proud!'

My family has always been close. I was born in 1973, twelve years after my big brother, Gavin, and seven years after my sister, Anne Marie. My little brother Norman is a year younger than me, and Garth, the baby of the family, is three years younger.

My full name is actually Catherine Astrid Salome Freeman. Mum originally wanted to call me Yasmin, but she changed her mind after I was born. She said that for some reason, as soon as she saw me she just knew I was a Catherine. I get Astrid from an aunt, and Salome was the name of an elderly Torres Strait Islander lady who used to be our neighbour.

'Make sure you name the baby after me,' Salome would say whenever she saw my mum. So, of course, my mother did.

The name Catherine is Greek for 'pure'. My second name, Astrid, is German for 'star'. Salome is a Hebrew name that means 'peace'. All my life, to my mother and my whole family, I've been known as Catherine – not Cathy. Mum sometimes calls me Catherina, but that's her only other name for me. It wasn't until 1990, after winning my first gold medal, that a journalist decided to re-name me Cathy. The name has stuck ever since.

It's never bothered me, but Mum can't stand it. 'If I wanted your name to be Cathy, I would've called you Cathy,' she says.

My cousin Roya feels the same way. 'Urrrgh! Cathy?' she says. 'That's not you. You're not Cathy, you're Catherine!'

That's our family – always sticking up for each other.

I had so much fun growing up. My younger brothers and I did everything together and I think that's the way Mum wanted it. We lived in a beautiful sunny place in Queensland called Mackay. I loved the hot weather and used to run around everywhere in bare feet. Even now when I go for a run on really hot days, it reminds me of growing up in Mackay – especially when I'm jogging on grass ovals. I can smell the scent of melaleuca and eucalyptus trees, just like I did when I was young. My face still sweats like it did in tropical Queensland, and my legs still love to run. I still feel as free as I did then.

My parents weren't rich, but that didn't matter to us – as long as we could go out and play, we were happy. We lived in a small, three-bedroom house at the bottom of Burston Street. My oldest brother, Gavin, had his own room, but I had to share a bedroom with Norm and Garth. We also didn't have a car or a telephone. I never complained about it, although some days at school I'd see kids buying meat pies and sausage rolls from the tuckshop and wish I could do the same.

'Mum,' I said one night, 'why can't we buy our lunches from the tuckshop like everyone else? Why do we have to be different?'

'Because it costs money, Catherine,' Mum said in her usual direct way. 'And anyway, it's bad for you.'

I decided to push my luck a bit further. 'But why do the other kids get to do it?'

'Catherine, can you go and get your brothers, please? It's time for dinner.' This was Mum's clever way of distracting me so I'd forget to worry about being different. It always worked.

Mum was really fussy about the food we ate. She was born on Palm Island (I call her my island girl!), so she grew up eating natural foods like fruit and fish. Junk food was pretty much a 'no go' in our family – there were never any lollies or chips in the cupboards at home. And Mum always made sure our school lunches were something healthy. She'd send us off in the morning with a wholemeal ham-and-cheese sandwich, an apple and a muesli bar packed into a brown paper bag.

Our school was called St Joseph's, but we called it St Joey's. Mackay had a fairly big population of Indigenous people so about one-third of the students were Aboriginal or Torres Strait Islander.

On my very first day, I couldn't get over how many kids were crying because they had to leave their mums.

'Ma, what's wrong with those kids?' I asked. 'Why are they crying so much?'

Even when I was little I wasn't one to cry in public, and here were all these kids bawling their eyes out. I'd never seen anything like it.

My best friend in kindy was a girl called Sharlene. She had long brown hair that flowed all the way down her back. She also had lots of freckles and a nose that crinkled up whenever she smiled.

One day we were in the toilet block when Sharlene let out the highest of high-pitched squeals.

'Sharlene,' I called out, 'is everything all right?'

'There's a frog!' she yelled.

I ran into her cubicle to have a look for myself. Sure enough, there in the toilet bowl was a huge green frog. Sharlene and I started giggling. Things like that were always happening in Mackay. My brothers and I would often see frogs, cane toads and lizards around the place.

St Joey's was Catholic so it had a church as part of the school. The church was fairly new, and had beautiful stained-glass windows that let in the light. It was such a serene place. All the students had to attend regularly so I ended up spending quite a bit of time there. Even now when I'm in Mackay I'm always happy to drop in for a visit, because it makes me feel at peace.

The church was where I celebrated my first communion. All the family were there, including my nanna. It was a bright sunny day, and I wore a beautiful white dress and a veil. I also had these gloriously white pull-up socks with little frills on the top. The socks matched my oh-so-shiny black shoes that I swear you could see your own reflection in!

Religion meant a lot to our family. Mum was raised Catholic, and then became a Baha'i before I was born. The Baha'i religion teaches that all people, no matter what their race or nationality, are equal. This idea makes sense to Mum. When she was young she went to a church where the white people sat up the front and the black people sat up the back. 'I knew it wasn't right,' she told me. 'Faith is meant to be about love and equality.'

Mum taught us two prayers to say every night before we went to sleep. One began like this: 'Oh God, guide me and protect me, illuminate the lamp of my heart and make me a brilliant star...' The second prayer was about easing the troubles in our lives. Whenever I was worried about something, Mum would tell me to 'leave it in God's hands'.

Not that I had too many worries – I was pretty happy and easygoing. Every day after school, my brothers and I would race home to play with the Sabatini kids. The Sabatinis were a Torres Strait

Islander family who lived in the house behind ours. I could walk less than five minutes from my front door and find lots of kids with the same background as me. We'd ride our bikes together and play games like chasey, murder in the dark and hide-and-seek. We felt comfortable with each other because we shared the same culture.

On the hill at the top end of our street were all the big brick houses with pools – that was where the white people lived. I thought that all white people were rich, and that anyone who had a car, a telephone or even carpet must be a millionaire. There was another girl in our street called Catherine and her house was on the hill. She had beautiful blonde hair and blue eyes and went to a private school. I used to watch her walk past to the bus stop and think how different our lives must be. While I was out running around in the dirt with my brothers, she was probably playing with dolls or make-up.

On the weekends we mostly hung out with our cousins. Mum didn't really like us to spend time outside of school with people who weren't family. We didn't care – the sleepovers we had at Nanna's were the best. Mum and Nanna and the aunties would go and play bingo together, leaving Auntie Karen to look after us. Karen was fairly young, so the boys would just run riot. As soon as she got us to bed – some of us on mattresses on the floor, some of us on the couch – we'd start telling spooky ghost stories. One night I was so scared I wouldn't even get up to go to the toilet.

On Saturdays we'd have barbecues together down by the harbour. The adults would sit on fold-up chairs or on blankets on the ground, and they'd talk and laugh and share news with one another. Us kids would play chasey in the playground. By the time the adults started serving out the sausages, chops, salads and drinks, we'd be starving.

Afterwards, we'd go back to running around like crazy. Things could get pretty wild when the cousins were all together. Every now and again, someone would fall over and there would be tears. But I never got caught and I never cried once. I was always happy when I was running.

And I was fast!

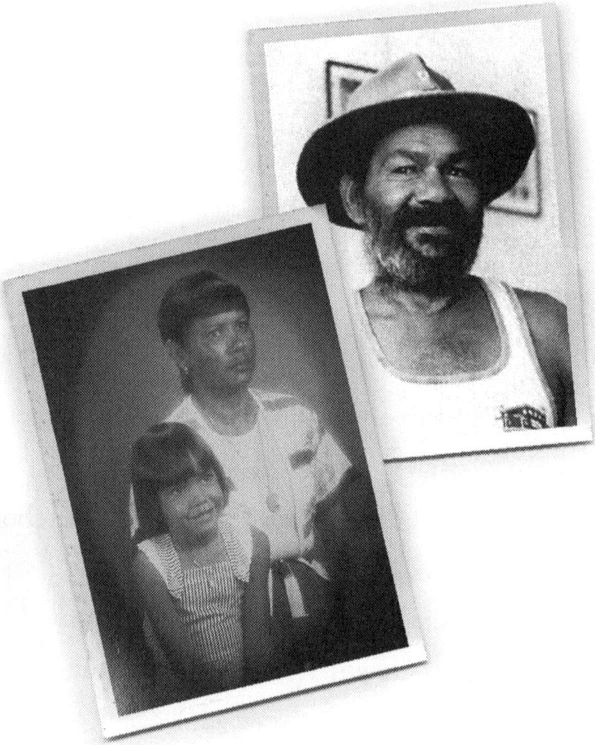

CHAPTER 2
My Family + Me

Mum says I got my sporting abilities from Dad. He was one of the best Rugby League players in Queensland, a real natural athlete. He played the game with such style and flair that his team-mates called him 'Twinkle Toes'.

I adored my dad. I remember one time when I was about two years old and he showed me a 'trick' with a fern leaf.

'Hey, Catherine, have a look at this!' he said.

As I watched, Dad reached out and touched the tip of a fern leaf with his finger. It curled up instantly and then slowly reopened. I thought it was like magic.

Every Sunday, my brothers and I would go down to the oval to watch Dad play rugby. Those hot afternoons were full of colour and activity. Dad's team was the Magpies so Norm and Garth would dress from head to toe in black and white.

The men who played rugby took the game very seriously. As I was a girl, going anywhere near the men's dressing rooms was strictly out of bounds. But sometimes curiosity got the better of me. When I saw my chance, I'd poke my head around the corner of the door to get a glimpse of life in a men's locker room. I remember the sound of the footy boots clanging on the cement floor and the smell the 'Deep Heat' body rub the players used. I felt a bit like a journalist or a detective whenever I got that close to the action.

Sport wasn't the only thing Dad and I had in common. We also loved to laugh. My dad was one of the funniest people around. I remember talking to him on the phone one time and having sore tummy muscles for days afterwards because I'd been laughing so hard. We were talking about the weather.

'It's raining cats and dogs, Catherine,' Dad said. 'Really. I can see them falling from the sky. Cats and dogs!'

That was my dad, always being silly. He had such a way about him, he could have convinced the whole world it really *was* raining cats and dogs.

When I was only five years old, Dad went away. At first Mum didn't tell us why he'd left, or even where he'd gone. She believed that you should accept things in life without questioning or judging. Besides, she was too busy taking care of us kids to sit around and get upset. 'Catherine,' she'd tell me, 'you've just got to get on with things and that's that.'

Mum arranged for us to go and see Dad every Christmas. He was a stockman and he'd gone to live on a cattle station at Woorabinda in central Queensland. The first year we visited, Dad taught us how to ride the horses on the property. I was only six, but Dad lifted me onto a horse and showed me how to hold the reins.

A few years later, I found out my parents had got a divorce. It was a shock, but at the time I didn't get too upset. I'm like Mum that way – I just try to make the best of things.

Mum's had a lot to deal with in her life, including not having our older sister, Anne-Marie, live at home with us. Just before I was born, Mum was told she had to put my sister into care. Mum was heartbroken, but she knew that's where Anne-Marie would get the best treatment.

Anne-Marie was born with something called cerebral palsy, which affects the way your brain works. There are different types of cerebral palsy, but Anne-Marie's condition was pretty severe. She didn't have much muscle control, so she couldn't run or jump or do any of the things I loved doing. Often when I was out chasing around after my brothers I'd think about how lucky I was.

We only got to visit Anne-Marie about three or four times a year. We'd hop on the train and travel for more than three hours to get to the hospital in

North Rockhampton. When we first got to Anne-Marie's room, my brothers and I would hang back. Anne-Marie couldn't sit up by herself so she had to be strapped into her wheelchair with thick leather belts. Her wrists were all bony like a bird and her feet looked contorted and twisted out of shape.

But my sister had so much spirit and personality that after a while I'd forget about her disabilities. Whenever she saw Mum, her whole face would light up in excitement. Anne-Marie couldn't talk, but she knew how to express herself. One day my auntie Lizzie was encouraging Anne-Marie to show her some affection. 'Come on,' she said. 'Show me some love.' Straightaway Anne-Marie started throwing her arms around wildly. She was trying to give Auntie Lizzie a hug.

With Dad gone, Mum found a job as a cleaner at the local high school so she could support us. Being a cleaner was the only thing Mum had ever been trained to do, but I never heard her complain about it. She'd had to leave school when she was fifteen because the laws in Australia at the time wouldn't allow her to continue. No one thought it was important for Aboriginal people to finish school or get a higher education in those days. Even so, my mum is one of the wisest and smartest people I know.

Every morning she'd get up at 6.30 a.m. to make our lunches, then go and clean at North Mackay High School for a few hours, and be back in time to wake us up and get us off to school as well. At the end of the day my brothers and I would trudge back up to the high school with her. North Mackay was very hilly; I reckon we walked some of the longest and steepest streets of Mackay on those afternoons.

Looking back, I kind of enjoyed hanging out with Mum, helping her clean. I liked the idea that we were making the world (or at least the school) a better place. There's something really satisfying about scrubbing a mark off a wall or vacuuming tiny bits of paper off the carpet. Mum took such pride in her work – she was a real perfectionist. Everything had to be done 'just so'. If I got a bit lazy, she'd soon let me know.

'Catherina,' she'd say, 'you missed a spot!'

Together we'd roll up our sleeves and pull back our hair and get down to the business of cleaning. But we could never rely on the boys for help, so Mum would send them outside to play. 'Go on,' she'd say, 'you boys get out in the fresh air.'

Without a word, my brothers would race off to the nearest playground. About halfway through Mum's shift, I'd head out to check up on them.

I loved my brothers, but they were always getting into trouble. Norman was really accident-prone. When we were little and had baths together, he'd always try to climb out of the tub. Once he even fell and cracked his head open on the hard bathroom tiles. Garth was a cutie – I called him my 'baby' – but he was completely hyperactive. When Auntie Lizzie babysat for us she used to tie a stocking around his leg and attach the other side to hers in order to stop him getting away.

Now that she was raising us on her own, Mum worked extra hard to make our lives as stable and normal as possible. Gav was the oldest so he took over Dad's role as man of the house. He was really protective of his younger sister and brothers, but especially of Mum. It was just the five of us and we thought that's how it would stay.

Then one day when I was about six years old, a man called Bruce Barber came into our lives. He'd met my mum at a Baha'i prayer meeting and started visiting our house on weekends.

One morning, I was standing in the yard when I saw his blue Holden pull up in our drive. 'Mum!' I yelled, running inside. 'That white man is here!'

My brothers and I didn't like Bruce much. If I came home from school and saw him in the lounge room, the first words out of my mouth were always, 'What's *he* doing here?'

We didn't know what to make of this stranger. He looked a bit like the Bush Tucker Man with his blond hair and scruffy beard. He was never loud or rude to us, but we hated the idea of someone replacing our dad.

One afternoon, we were driving in Bruce's car when I saw Mum slide along to sit closer to him in the front seat. I got so angry. Who did this guy think he was? It seemed wrong that Mum was sitting that close to another man. To make her move away,

I started poking her under the seat with my foot.

'Who's kicking?' she said, turning round to look at us. 'Who's doing that?'

My brothers and I just giggled and said nothing. We all felt the same way.

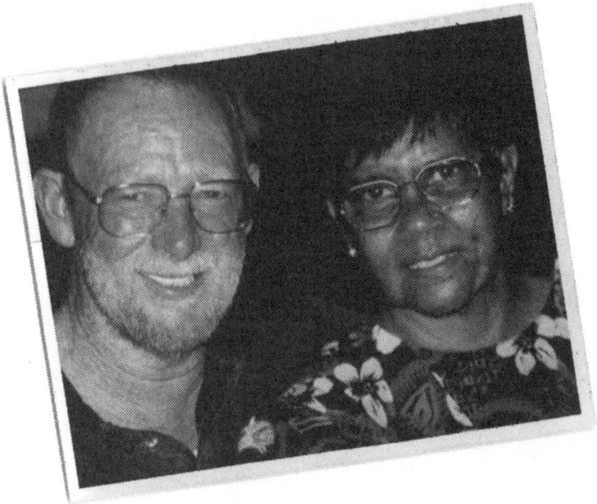

CHAPTER 3
New Dad

'Hey, kids,' Bruce said, 'I've got something to tell you.'

We were driving to a friend's house when Bruce stopped the car and turned round to face us. I was nine years old and Bruce had been dating Mum for about three years. He took a deep breath, then blurted out, 'Your mum and I are getting married.'

I couldn't believe it. Married! Surely Mum would have told us? And what about Dad?

Straightaway, I started to worry about how he would feel once he heard the news. I was so angry with Mum. What did she think she was doing? I just wanted things to go back to the way they had been before Bruce came along. If he and Mum got married, it meant there'd be no chance my parents would get back together.

I knew my brothers agreed with me. Gavin even made a trip out to Woorabinda to tell Dad what was going on. But it didn't make any difference. Mum had made up her mind. She was going to marry Bruce Barber and she was confident it would be the best thing for all of us.

The wedding was to take place at the house of one of our friends. Despite my feelings about Bruce, I was pretty excited about the chance to get all dressed up. I was a bit of a tomboy so this didn't happen very often. I did have one or two dolls and a few other girly things, but mostly I preferred getting around in T-shirts and shorts to wearing frilly dresses.

When the wedding day arrived, I put on a red dress and strappy white shoes and felt really grown up. Mum looked so pretty in her apricot dress, sheer white stockings and white shoes. Whenever she got dressed up, I thought my mum was the most beautiful woman in the whole world. On the day of her wedding, it was like she'd transformed from a cleaning lady into a radiant queen.

Even my little brothers looked tidy for once. Their shirts were tucked in and they wore long pants and shiny lace-up shoes. They looked so neat and respectable at the start of the ceremony, but by the end they resembled messy little monsters again. Luckily they didn't do anything too mischievous to spoil Mum's special day.

Mum looked so happy. She danced the night away with her new husband. Our friends had prepared a feast for the event and the food smelled amazing. I ended up in the backyard, watching my brothers run around the madmen. I wondered how much our lives would change now that we had a step-dad.

I didn't have to wait long to find out. Less than a year after the wedding, Bruce was offered a new job in Hughenden in far north-west Queensland. The whole family had to pack up and move from Mackay to a place hundreds of kilometres away. Suddenly, all I'd ever known for the first ten years of my life was completely gone. The warmth of my nanna, the fun times with my cousins, and the familiarity and security of everything I'd grown up with. It was such a big change, and while I didn't complain about it at the time, I resented Bruce. He was the reason we'd had to leave Mackay. He'd met my mother, married her and then made all of us move. It didn't seem fair.

Hughenden was home to red desert, scrubby bush, coal trains – and not much else. As soon as we arrived, Mum enrolled my brothers and me at St Francis, the local Catholic primary school. It was a small school with only forty or so students. We weren't the only black kids, but there were less than there had been at Mackay.

The school actually wasn't that bad. It had a pet sheep and sometimes while I was in class I'd look out the window and see it wandering around outside. I was in fourth grade and my teacher, Mr Larkin,

Age four

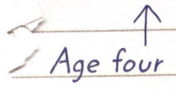

Notice I'm smiling in every photo. That's because life is good!

Age six

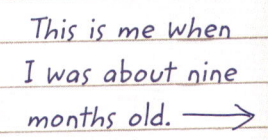

This is me when I was about nine months old. →

Here's my dad, →
the first man I ever loved.
I got my running
ability from him.

This is me at age four with Mum. Doesn't Mum look beautiful? My hair wasn't normally that neat!

My greatest inspiration — my big sister, Anne-Marie.

This is my brothers and me at Bruce and Mum's wedding in Mackay. That's Norm on the left and Garth on the right.

This is me at ten. Check out the big bows in my hair!

This is my Queensland team uniform. Yep, I'm still smiling!

This is me with my friend Maggie when we were eleven. We represented Queensland together.

This is me in high school. Even when I was competing, I always ran for the love of it.

My first Commonwealth Games gold medal. Here I am with Monique Dunstan, Kerry Johnson and Kathy Sambell (left to right). We won the 100m relay race. ☆ Extra special! ☆

A rare photo of my brother and me at the track. That's Norm on the left.

Here I am at sixteen with my great coach and mentor Mike.

My first Olympic Games in 1992 in Barcelona. I ran in the 400m relay race. A huge learning experience.

This is Melinda Gainsford-Taylor and me at the 1994 Commonwealth Games in Victoria, Canada. We're celebrating my gold medal and her bronze medal in the 200m final. Don't we look happy?!

My first public acknowledgement of my pride in being Indigenous. This is me celebrating my 400m gold medal at the 1994 Commonwealth Games.

This is one of my favourite running shots. I'm training in Atlanta, a few months before the 1996 Olympics. A lot of hard work went into this body! ⟶

This is me with my dog Frankie in 1992. We did almost everything together — he even came to training with me in my backpack!

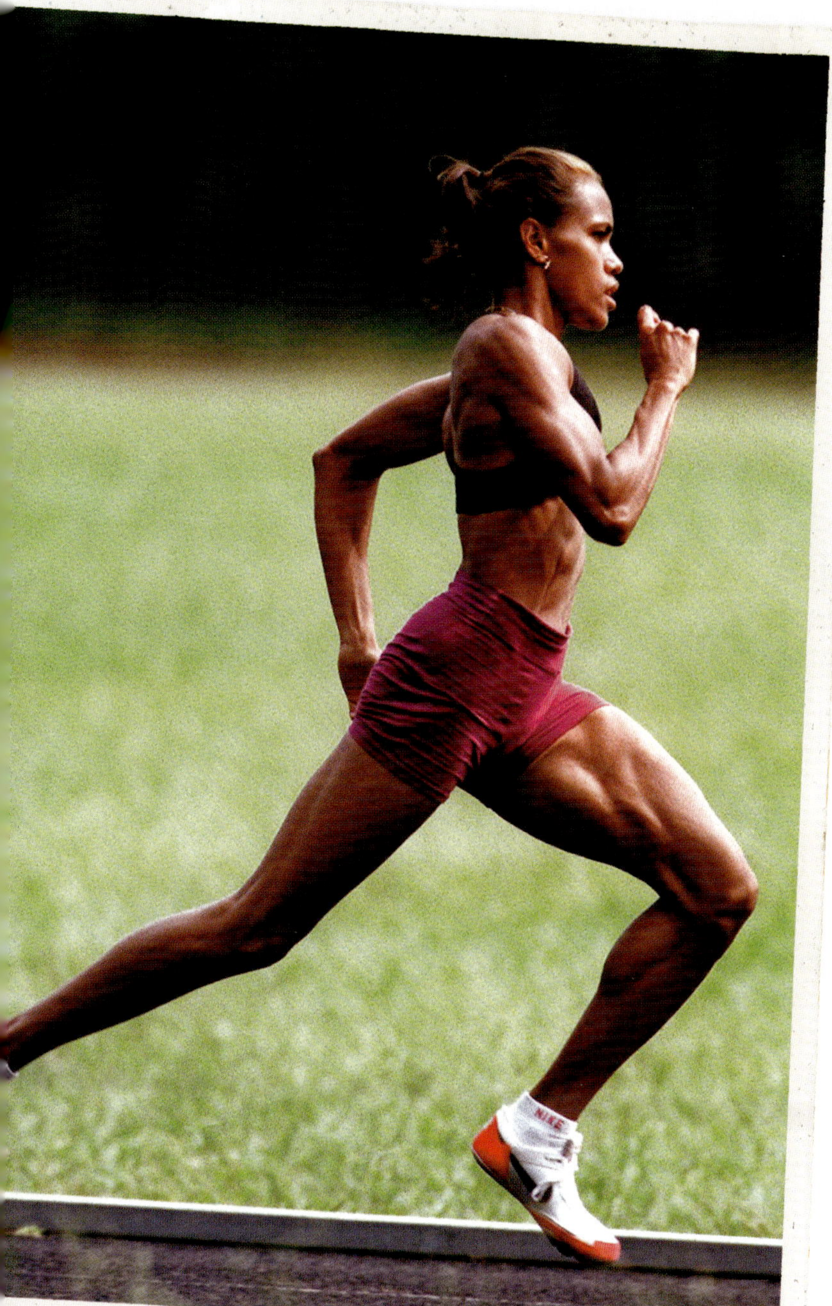
NIKE

The 1996 Olympic 400m final in Atlanta is regarded as one of the best women's 400m races ever. I ran the fastest I've ever run in this race, and it felt amazing!!

If there was one competitor who had my fullest respect, it was this lady — Marie-José Pérec. Here we are at the 1996 Olympics. She won the gold, and I got the silver.

Even though I didn't win gold at the Atlanta Olympics, I still felt like a champion.

loved Banjo Patterson. He made us learn the poems 'The Geebung Polo Club' and 'The Man From Ironbark'. He taught us so well, I can still remember those poems now.

Each morning at assembly all the students had to march in time to the recording of a trumpet. I always walked next to my friends Susan and Bec. The three of us used to wear these big blue ribbons in our hair. When I look at photos of us now it makes me laugh – those ribbons were almost bigger than our heads! I also had a secret crush on a boy called Richard. I thought he was the most handsome boy in the whole school.

St Francis had a tuckshop where you could get 'cold cups' – frozen cups of cordial that cost fifty cents each. My favourites were the red ones, which were so strong they made your lips and tongue completely red. We also used to eat the apples that grew on a tree in the school grounds. They were small, brown, sticky and sweet. It was fun to just pick one and eat it whenever you were hungry.

It was in Hughenden that I realised I might have been wrong about Bruce. I couldn't help noticing how kind and friendly he was, or how much he made my mum laugh. Little by little, I came to see that he cared about all of us, not just Mum.

His special nickname for me was 'Min Min Light'. No one really knows where the Min Min Light comes from, but it's a mysterious glow that people sometimes see in the desert at night. I've never seen it, but apparently it moves across the sky at an incredible speed. That's why Bruce thought it was the perfect name for me.

He was really impressed by the way I'd started to win more and more ribbons at my school athletics carnivals. Our house was near the river so he'd get my brothers and me to practise doing sprints up and down the sandbanks. Norm and Garth would usually muck around and not do it properly, but I always tried to do exactly what Bruce said. The dried-out river was sandy and heavy to run in, so we had to pump our arms that little bit extra to get anywhere. It was also hard work for our legs, but more fun than running on the school oval.

We always ran in bare feet. Naturally, the boys – especially Norman – were faster than me, but I enjoyed chasing after them. I can still see the brown legs of my youngest brother, Garth, digging into the ground and flicking up little fountains of sand behind him. If I was chasing him, I'd get a face full of gritty, grainy bits!

Bruce saw how much I loved to run. Pretty soon he had me training three times a week at the local high school. He'd sit in the school's rickety old grandstand and watch as I ran twelve laps of a 400m sawdust track.

I still remember the first time we went. It was late afternoon and I just kept going round in lane one, my bare feet kicking up the red dust. The late-afternoon light in the middle of summer was magical, and I didn't have a care in the world. Even after I'd run more than ten laps I didn't feel tired – just happy and free.

It's hard to explain the feeling I got from running. I was so quiet and shy that most of the time I let my running do the talking for me. It allowed me to express myself. I'd lose myself in this personal space where I felt safe and strong, like I was the only person in the world.

Of course, it wasn't always like that. I still went through phases where I didn't want to train. One day Mum told me to go and get ready, but I just lay on my bed and pretended to be asleep. I was sick of not being able to play with my friends as much as I wanted. Finally Mum barged into my room.

'It's time to go, Catherine. Come on!'

'Mum, I don't want to go,' I said. 'I don't want to do this any more.'

Mum grabbed hold of my arm. I knew she was really mad. 'I wish you were Anne-Marie,' she said. 'Look, you know your sister can't walk, can't talk, she can't do all the things that you can. You've got two good arms and two good legs, now go out there and use them.'

I stared at Mum in shock, but she was right. I knew I owed it to Anne-Marie to be the best that I could be. I got out of bed and never complained about training again.

CHAPTER 4
World's Greatest Athlete

'Catherine, how'd you go?' Bruce and Mum asked as soon as I walked in the door.

I'd just got back from the country zone athletics titles in Mt Isa. I'd competed in the 100m, the 200m, the relay, the long jump and the high jump.

'I won four out of my five events,' I said.

Bruce looked so happy and Mum jumped straight up and gave me a hug.

'So come on, then,' said Bruce, 'where are your medals?'

'I didn't get any,' I told him. 'Just certificates.'

Bruce frowned. 'You should have got medals.'

I shrugged. 'I think some of the other girls got them.'

A few weeks later, Bruce found out that the white girls who'd come second to me had been given my medals. He was furious, but he tried not to let it show.

'Don't worry, Catherine,' he said, 'nobody can take away the fact that you won those races fair and square.'

The more I raced, the more I loved to win, but not everyone was happy about it. I began to notice the dirty looks I was getting from some of the Hughenden mothers when the new Aboriginal kid in town kept beating their girls.

Although I've never felt that different to anyone else in this country, I think a lot of Indigenous Australians are made to feel like they don't belong here. And that's called racism. There were examples of it in my own family. My grandfather, a talented

Rugby League player, wasn't allowed to represent Australia because of the colour of his skin. And my nanna was taken away from her Aboriginal mother when she was just eight years old because her father was a white man. She was sent to a government mission and didn't see her mother again until she was a teenager. She's part of what's known as the stolen generation.

Because my nanna wasn't allowed to live as a traditional Aborigine, the road ended for us in terms of our Indigenous culture. My brothers and I don't know any Aboriginal languages and we weren't brought up with Dreaming stories. It's only now that I'm starting to learn about the Aboriginal creation stories that get handed down from generation to generation.

I grew up around a lot of adults who'd experienced racism and had low self-esteem as a result. This had a big effect on how my brothers and I saw ourselves. There were times when we'd be too embarrassed to go into a room full of white people. At school, kids would tease us about being Aboriginal. 'Ew, yuck! You eat witchetty grubs,' they'd say.

One time we were on holidays in Sydney when I had a run-in with a shopkeeper. We'd been out sightseeing and Bruce had just gone to buy us some lunch. I was standing in front of a florist's shop when this lady came out and told me to move.

'Get away from here! I don't want people like you standing there,' she said.

'What?' I replied, and rushed over to Mum and Bruce. He asked me what had happened. 'She told me to get away from her shop,' I said. I was quite calm, but Mum sure wasn't and neither was Bruce. He went over and said something to the woman.

'Well, how would you like it if I came and stood in front of your place?' she yelled at him.

'You're quite welcome,' he said. 'I'll give you my address and you can come and stand in front of my place every day.'

The woman stormed back into her shop and that was that. I decided not to let it bother me. It wasn't in my personality to get upset about stuff like that.

When I turned eleven we moved again – this time to a place called Moura, which is a hundred kilometres west of Rockhampton. Moura was known for its cotton fields, and it was a lot greener and prettier than dry, dusty Hughenden. On the way there, I remember looking out the window of our blue Holden and seeing all these white balls of cotton moving through the air like giant flakes of snow. Our new house was surrounded by beautiful wattle trees. Between the bright golden wattle and the snowy cotton fields, it felt like we'd moved to some kind of fairytale land.

Mum soon found a job as a cleaner at the local hardware store and sometimes I'd go along to help. If my little brothers came too, it was my job to keep an eye on them. Not that they'd always listen to me. Half the time they'd be running around as if some kind of inner aliens had taken over their bodies.

After only nine months, Bruce found another job in a tiny town called Coppabella. It was our third move in two years. Our new house was right by the railway, and at night I would lie awake listening to the sounds of the massive coal trains as they rumbled past.

I was still going in athletics competitions, but Mum thought it was important to try lots of different things so she enrolled Norm and me in karate. Mum and Bruce thought it would be good for us – especially for my brother. They wanted us to learn discipline through self-defence.

The hall where we had lessons had waxy wooden floors, a high ceiling and louvred windows that let in the sunlight and the breeze. I soon learnt that karate was very different from running. When I ran I often felt wild and free, but in karate the positioning of your body had to be exact or you weren't doing it right. The lessons were all about order and structure, and there was the added pressure to perform well in front of the other kids in the class. If you weren't doing the same thing as everyone else, the teacher would single you out in a loud voice. At times I'd be practising when I'd hear: 'Catherine! Your kicks aren't high enough. Ten push-ups, please. Now!'

One afternoon we were being tested to see what grade we should be in. Norm and I started doing the moves and I got quite enthusiastic about it. I thought I was doing well, and let fly with an energetic kick aimed at Norman's chest. Unfortunately, my leg went too high and my toe got Norm straight in the eye! He dropped to the floor like a stone and lay there, groaning in agony. I felt so bad! What had I done?

'Norm! Are you all right?' I kept saying. Some parents came over and took him away so they could check on his injury. The teacher told me I had to stay where I was and finish my test. He put me with a girl who already had a black belt.

For the rest of the afternoon, I couldn't stop worrying about Norm. Was he okay? What if I'd blinded him? Norm was fine, but I was so distracted I did really poorly in my test.

Not that it mattered in the end – we had to stop karate when we moved back to Mackay later that year. I was so happy to be home; I couldn't wait to catch up with all my cousins. I was twelve years old and loved horse riding and going to the beach. But my biggest love was still my running.

Norm was also competing in more and more races. For the national and state titles, we'd have to travel to places like Melbourne and Brisbane.

We still didn't have much money, but Bruce always found a way so we didn't have to miss out. He even started selling lamingtons door to door to pay for our trips.

He also talked to us about the importance of setting goals. 'You've got to make your dreams stick in your subconscious,' he said. Bruce often used words like 'subconscious', and other phrases like 'mental rehearsal', 'self-talk' and 'self-conviction'. I'm not sure I totally understood, but I listened and took notice. I had a dream to win a gold medal at the Olympics one day and I wanted to make it real.

Bruce encouraged me to make a certificate or a poster for my wall, something that would inspire me. All on my own I came up with the sentence: 'I am the world's greatest athlete'. Bruce said that if I read the words every day, they would sink into my subconscious, which is the most powerful part of the mind. Once my mind had accepted the words, then my body would act to make sure they came true.

I found a piece of cardboard and a big black marker pen and wrote in bold capital letters:

I AM THE WORLD'S GREATEST ATHLETE

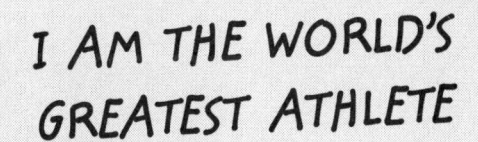

Then I stuck the certificate on my bedroom wall, right opposite my bed. It was the first thing I saw when I woke up every morning, and the last thing I saw before I fell asleep at night.

'You don't even have to read the words,' Bruce told me. 'Just looking at them will be enough for them to sink into your subconscious.'

It turns out that Bruce was right. There were some weeks when I would look at my certificate up to twenty times a day. And the more I looked, the more convinced I became that one day I was going to be an Olympic champion.

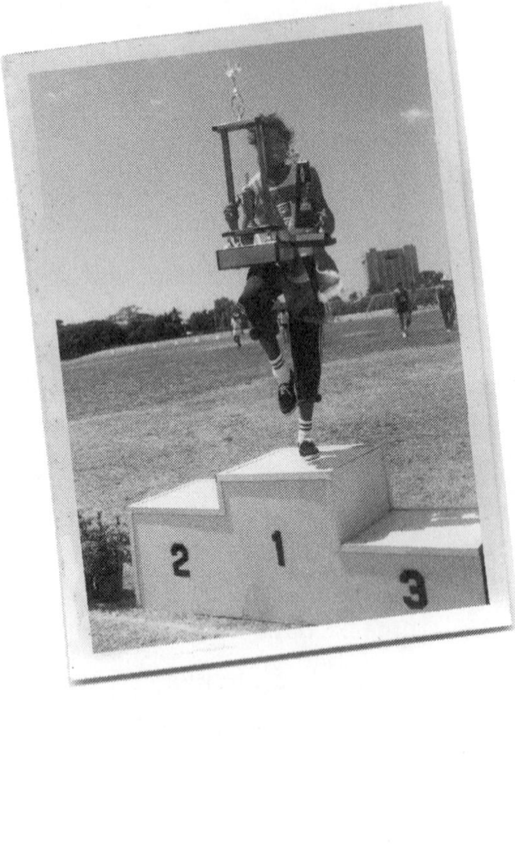
2
1
3

CHAPTER 5
School Days

'Hey, Catherine, how would you feel about going to boarding school?'

Bruce's question caught me by surprise. I was fourteen years old and I'd been going to the local high school in Andergrove, Mackay. I was so shy I used to wear a cap to school every day so no one could see my face. But if my parents thought that boarding school was a good idea, then it was okay with me. Who knows, I thought, it might even be interesting. Little did I know what I was getting myself into!

The headmaster at my old school arranged for me to get a scholarship to Fairholme College, an exclusive girls' school in Toowoomba. Toowoomba is a city in south-east Queensland, about two hours' drive from Brisbane.

The day I left good old Mackay and the safety of my wonderful family was the day I left home forever. We didn't realise it at the time, but I would never live with my parents full-time again. We packed up all my things and piled into the car for the long trip south to Toowoomba. As we drove through the school's massive front gates, I couldn't get over how big and old the buildings were. Bruce parked our dusty Holden right next to a shiny Mercedes Benz. I had never seen anything like this place before, but I wasn't scared or nervous, I was more intrigued.

The school principal, Mr Faragher, met us in the entrance courtyard. Although he said hello and shook hands with Bruce, he didn't seem overly warm or friendly. I thought he looked like the serious type.

'Come this way,' he said, and led us into his office. Bruce started talking straightaway about my running abilities. He was really excited that I'd get the chance to train with one of Australia's best coaches, Paul Faithful, while I was at Fairholme.

Mr Faragher looked from Bruce to me and frowned. 'We have some rules and regulations at this school, Catherine,' he said. 'It may have been different at your old school, but here at Fairholme, hair colour is not permitted.'

He was talking about the grey streaks in my dark-brown hair. I'd spent the week before doing work experience at a hairdresser's and thought it would be fun to experiment a little. Apparently, this wasn't allowed at Fairholme.

My new school had a long list of rules. No more would I be free to dye my hair or paint my nails any colour I wanted. Fairholme girls were only allowed to wear two types of earrings (studs or sleepers), and their school uniforms had to be knee-length or longer. They even had to wear the same types of bows in their hair. It was definitely a change from the relaxed life I had enjoyed back in Mackay.

I shared a room with three other girls. It was your typical boarding-school bedroom: the curtains were old and faded, and the carpet wasn't anything to write home about, either. The bed linen was plain white, but at least we got to have our own towels. We also had our own cupboards and drawer space. Some of the bigger rooms had mirrors and hand basins, but we had to share a bathroom with the other girls on our level of the dorm.

I soon learnt that boarding school was all about routine. Every moment of your day was organised, with no room for anything else unless you got permission first. Dinner was at the same time every night in the huge communal dining room. We sat about ten girls to a table and helped ourselves to food from a buffet. It actually wasn't too bad. We even got to eat desserts like ice-creams, puddings and jelly. At home we'd only eaten desserts on special occasions.

Besides the dining room, my favourite place to hang out was the common room. This was where

I went to relax and watch TV, listen to music, read books or just chat to friends. Spending time in the common room was fun, and it made me forget about my homesickness. It was hard to be away from my family, especially in a place that was so different to Mackay.

First of all there was the weather. Summers in Mackay were generally hot and humid, with temperatures in the 30s and winters no colder than around 15°C. In Toowoomba it could get as cold as 5°C – quite a bit cooler than I was used to. My first year at Fairholme was a real test. In the winter I wore tracksuit pants rolled up under my school uniform to try to keep warm.

The lifestyle in Toowoomba was also really different. Mackay's tropical climate made it very laid-back. They say the tropics make people 'go troppo' – they live and work at a slower pace. It's nice. Toowoomba certainly didn't have the same tropical, holiday feel and the people were much more conservative.

My first term at Fairholme was ten weeks long. After only a month, ten weeks started to feel like forever. One night I called Mum and we both ended up in tears.

'Mum, I want to come home,' I cried into the phone. I felt so sad and alone. All I wanted was to be hugged by my mum. 'You have to come get me.'

'Darling, of course I'll come get you,' Mum said. 'Everything will be okay.'

I found out later that Mum had hung up the phone and marched straight to Bruce. 'I'm getting on the first bus down there and bringing her straight home,' she told him.

But Bruce put his foot down. He knew that I'd be better off at Fairholme, especially in terms of my running. Eventually he talked Mum around.

He was right, but it was a huge adjustment. I missed coming home from school every day and seeing people smiling and laughing together, or singing and playing the guitar. None of the students seemed to smile much at Fairholme. They were too busy worrying about their grades or what other people thought of them. Some nights I cried myself to sleep, burying my face in the pillow so the other girls wouldn't hear.

I just didn't seem to fit in. For starters, I was the only Aboriginal girl at the school. Out of six hundred students there were only two other black girls – a boarder from Papua New Guinea and a day girl whose parents came from Africa. But it wasn't just the colour of my skin, my attitude was different, too. Most of the girls at Fairholme took school very seriously. The pressure to do well was so intense that many of them would break down if they got an A instead of an A+. They were obsessed by the idea of becoming doctors or lawyers or politicians.

I just wasn't like that. I spent a lot of time in class staring out the window in my own little dream world. I would have much rather been playing sport than sitting in a classroom. In terms of Cathy Freeman being a model 'A' student...well, I certainly wasn't!

There were a few girls at school who were more like me. They were usually country girls who were down-to-earth and easygoing. We weren't really part of the 'cool' crowd, but we were happy enough not to be. My closest friends were Lynne, Tania, Madonna and Donna.

Lynne was great fun. She and I once played a trick on our room-mate Roberta. Roberta was fairly serious so Lynne and I thought it would be fun to stir her up a bit. One day after class Lynne came up with a plan.

'Hey, Catherine,' she said, 'let's take Roberta's mattress out while she's not here. Come on!'

Together we pulled Roberta's mattress off its wooden frame. But once we'd dragged it out of the room, we realised we didn't have anywhere to put it.

'I know,' Lynne said. 'Let's hide it in the storeroom.'

We scurried down the hallway to the storeroom at the other end. With a mighty effort we threw the mattress into the dark room. Phew! I was so relieved when we'd closed the storeroom door.

Lynne and I got the giggles as we waited for Roberta to come back to our room. Unfortunately, she didn't think our joke was all that funny, and went straight to the head matron to dob us in. Next thing we knew we were being hauled down to her office.

'Catherine Freeman and Lynne West!' Miss Johnson yelled. 'What did you think you were doing?'

I was looking at my shoes, but Lynne spoke up. 'We didn't really mean any harm, Miss,' she said. 'It's not like anyone got hurt.'

As punishment, Miss Johnson put us on dining-room duties for a week. Lynne and I decided our prank had been worth it. Anything to break up the boring day-to-day routine of school life.

The weekends were better. One time I was invited to stay at Tania's place so that we could go horse riding. I loved horses – they reminded me of the Christmases we spent out at Woorabinda with Dad.

I feel so close to nature when I'm on a horse. Whether I'm just trotting or galloping at full speed, it always makes me happy. When I ride it's like I'm at one with the earth and the horse – I can feel the energy forces that come up off the ground. It's the same feeling as the one I get through the tips of my feet when I run. It's awesome – like flying.

The cheekiest girl in our group was definitely Madonna. Her family owned and ran a cattle property in central-western Queensland. She was a real cow-girl. She even took part in rodeos and used to ride bucking bulls!

Madonna was different to the other girls at Fairholme – she didn't like to conform. She was a tomboy who had a passion for jeans and hated wearing skirts or dresses. Some people saw her as a tough, smart-mouthed ratbag, but I thought she was great.

'You've got to live your life,' she used to tell me. 'Take the bull by the horns!'

Our friend Donna was also fairly wild. She once painted the principal's cat green. I can still remember the look on his stony face when he spoke to us about it at assembly.

'I'm absolutely disgusted,' he said, 'that someone at this school – some *criminal* – would do something like this. My cat could have been killed!'

We all stood there terrified. Before Donna could confess, the principal threatened to take away some of our privileges unless the culprit came forward. What a drama! Even though the principal was deadly serious, I couldn't help but see the funny side of the whole situation. Luckily, Donna had used water-based paint, so the poor cat wasn't harmed.

After a few months at Fairholme, I got the nickname 'Flowers'. My birthday is on the 16th of February, two days after Valentine's Day. That year my parents sent me a huge bunch of flowers, but they arrived a day early on the 15th. When I collected them from the office, I had to walk past a group of girls hanging out on the verandah.

'Hey, Catherine,' one of them called out, 'did someone send you flowers for Valentine's Day?'

'Oooh,' another girl chimed in, 'Catherine's got a boyfriend!'

They teased me for days afterwards, and from then on, my name wasn't Catherine Freeman any more, it was 'Flowers'!

The truth was I wasn't that interested in boys – I was too shy. In fact, I usually ran away from people of the opposite sex...I really did!

My first kiss had given me the biggest shock of my life. I was only nine years old and Mum had sent me out looking for Norm. After I'd trudged around the streets searching everywhere for him, I decided to check the house of one of his friends. Out of nowhere this boy planted a great big sloppy kiss on my lips. Yuck! I thought. How disgusting!

The next time someone tried to kiss me I was fifteen. We were at a school dance, and I kept shoving bread into my mouth so this boy wouldn't get the chance to kiss me. But it didn't work – he kissed me anyway!

Eventually I learnt to make the best of things at Fairholme. Sport helped. I was always training for one sport or another. If it wasn't running, it was basketball or touch football. My main rival in athletics was a girl called Kylie. We were always polite to each other, but I think the fact that I was faster than her got on her nerves. She'd been the top athlete at the school before I came along.

Even though I was winning races, the head coach didn't seem to take me that seriously. I got on better with one of the teachers, Mr Sessarago. Sess coached me in high jump and really believed in my talent. One day he gave me a framed black-and-white photograph of me high jumping. Underneath the picture, he'd written a message and also a quote from the former president of the United States, Franklin D. Roosevelt: *'The only limit to our realisation of tomorrow will be our doubts of today'.*

When the 1988 Olympics were on, Sess let the athletics team out of class so we could watch it on TV. I was fifteen and my two favourite runners were Carl Lewis and Florence Griffith-Joyner (also known as Flo Jo). As we watched them both win medals,

Sess turned to me. 'You'll be up there with those guys one day,' he said.

I couldn't believe it. I was used to hearing stuff like this from Bruce, but not from anyone else. To be told that I'd make it to the Olympics by someone who wasn't family meant a lot.

You'll be up there one day.

I couldn't get Sess's words out of my head.

CHAPTER 6
Bright Future

'Are we there yet?' I asked Sess.

We were driving to Nudgee College in Brisbane to watch my brother Norm compete in the athletics carnival. I didn't know it at the time, but my life was about to change forever.

Not long after we arrived, I was introduced to a man named Mike Danila. Mike was Romanian, and his greatest passion in life was athletics. He'd been living in Australia for less than five years when he was asked to become the coach at my brother's school. Norm was a talented runner, so Mike was convinced that I must be talented as well.

'So you're Norm's big sister,' he said. 'Are you as fast as he is?'

I shrugged. It was no secret in our family that Norm had way more natural ability than I did.

But then Sess spoke up. 'Flowers has lots of potential,' he said. 'I think she's got a really bright future.'

A few months after that meeting, Mike started coaching at Kooralbyn International School. Because of Mike's reputation, Bruce arranged for Norm and me to leave our schools and attend Kooralbyn instead. I was sixteen and I'd been at Fairholme for just over a year. Although I was excited by the thought of a new school, I also had doubts. What if I didn't like it? What if I didn't fit in?

I needn't have worried – Kooralbyn seemed like a fun place right from the start. The school was only ten years old and sat at the foothills of a beautiful mountain range. It was so peaceful. Right next door was the Kooralbyn Valley Resort, a fancy new hotel with a golf course and a polo field. The school only took two hundred and fifty students, and about thirty percent of them were from overseas. This meant that there were heaps of black kids from all over the place – Papua New Guinea, the Pacific Islands and even Cuba.

Kooralbyn was such a change from Fairholme. It was so relaxed, it made Fairholme seem like a high-security jail. We had a uniform, but you could wear it however you wanted – skirts could be as short as you liked and jewellery was allowed. The place just had a lot more 'soul'. It was easy to make friends, and students were encouraged to be individuals. There were also more international students. I made friends from Japan, France, Cuba, China and India.

One of my friends, Argo, came from Papua New Guinea. I was walking towards the school assembly hall one day when Argo snuck up behind me. He gave me a huge bear hug and picked me up off the ground.

'Argo!' I laughed. 'What are you up to?'

'I think we should become blood brother and sister,' he said.

I was touched that he'd chosen me. I watched as he took a sewing needle from his pocket and pricked his finger. Before I knew it, he'd pricked my finger, too. We pressed them together to signify that we were blood brother and sister forever.

Besides Argo, I had heaps of other friends – I even had a tall, cute boyfriend from France. He was in the year above me and his name was Laurent. I loved hearing him speak in French whenever he called home. But not everyone was happy about our relationship. Another girl in my year got really upset when she found out about us. Turns out I wasn't the only one who liked Laurent!

Some of my friends were also on the athletics team with me. Christine came from Queensland too, and she and I were room-mates as well as team-mates. She was a bit of a rebel and on the last day of school she convinced me to wag training with her.

'Come on, Cath,' she said. 'What's one day of training?'

'I guess so,' I said. 'But what about Mr Danila? You know he'll go nuts if he finds out.'

'Don't worry about it,' Christine said. 'He doesn't own us.'

We decided we'd better hide so we wouldn't get caught. There wasn't enough room for both of us under the bed so Christine hid there, while I hid in the cupboard.

We should have known we wouldn't get away with it. When Mike saw we weren't at training, he came and found us. He was furious!

'Where on earth have you been?' he said. 'I've been searching all over for you two!'

Mike told us he'd even jumped the fence and cut his leg while he was looking for us. Christine and I felt so bad. We knew Mike put his heart and soul into coaching. We apologised and from that day on, we never skipped training again.

It was at Kooralbyn that I got serious about athletics. With Mike as my coach, my running really took off. I'd never met anyone like him. He was just so full of life, enthusiasm and passion. He had the attitude that you had to work hard to achieve anything worthwhile. At Fairholme, I'd become lazy, training only two or three times a week. Kooralbyn had its own four-lane running track and Mike had us out there every day. Although we trained in a group, he always spent extra time with me, giving me encouragement and pushing me further. It didn't take long for my running times to improve.

One day a group of us were sitting around when Mike turned to me. 'You'd better start practising your signature,' he said.

'What for?' I asked.

'Soon you'll have to start writing hundreds of autographs.'

Mike told me he was thinking about entering me in the Commonwealth Games trials. We had a month to get ready.

'Do you think I'm good enough?' I asked.

Mike said he knew I could do it. It was hard not to catch his excitement.

The trials were held in Randwick in Sydney. I wasn't too nervous, but I knew it was an important day. This was my chance to represent Australia.

I was competing in two events – the 100m and the 200m. 'Just treat them like any other race,' Mike told me.

I ended up tying for third in the 100m and coming fifth in the 200m. I hadn't been expecting much, so I was happy with my performance. Mike seemed happy, too. He thought my times might be good enough to get me a place on the 100m relay team. He had such faith that I was going to be a famous athlete someday.

A few weeks after the trials, I woke up in my parents' house in Brisbane. I was on the top bunk of my double-decker bed, and Bruce was standing in front of me with a newspaper. He had it open to the page where they listed all the Commonwealth Games athletes. I grabbed it, and there was my name. I'd been chosen as one of the four runners in the women's 100m relay. It was awesome! I was only sixteen years old and I was going to the Commonwealth Games.

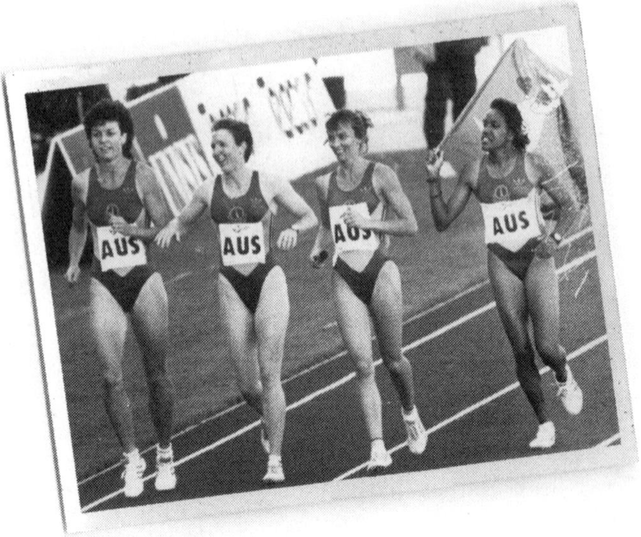
AUS
AUS
AUS
AUS

CHAPTER 7
Running for Australia

'Catherine, we're so proud of you,' Mum said. 'Have fun over there and make the most of it, you hear?'

Mum, Bruce and I were standing at the airport in Brisbane, waiting for my flight to be called. I was so excited. I couldn't wait to get to Auckland in New Zealand to compete in my first Commonwealth Games. At sixteen, I was the youngest member of the Australian athletics team.

Bruce gave me a hug goodbye. 'Go over there and sock it to them!' he said.

Mum waved to me all the way to the airport gate. 'Bye, darling,' she called out. 'And don't forget to ring.'

When I arrived in Auckland, I was taken straight to the Commonwealth Games village, my home for the next two weeks. The village was brand new, so it was really fresh and clean. My race wasn't on till the end of the Games, so I had heaps of spare time on my hands. As the days went by, I found myself sleeping lots, and eating too much as well. There was a huge dining room for all the athletes and you could eat as much chocolate cake, muffins and cheesecake as you liked. I pigged out and even took some mini-cheesecakes back to my room.

I was sharing a unit with Kathy Sambell and Monique Dunstan. At nineteen, Monique was the closest to me in age and we got on really well. I used to paint her nails for her with my bright-red nail polish.

Of course, I did have to do a bit of preparation for

the relay race as well. But even being at the warm-up track was a thrill. I kept seeing all these Olympic champions. I was in the same team as Debbie Flintoff-King, Robert de Castella, Steve Moneghetti and Darren Clarke. These guys were my idols – I had watched Debbie and Rob win gold medals on TV – so getting to see them up close was great.

One day Mike and I ran into the Jamaican sprinter Merlene Ottey. Merlene was one of the world's fastest women – by this stage she'd already won three Olympic medals. Mike was so excited to meet her. He told her he thought I was a champion of the future.

'Merlene, this is Catherine Freeman,' he said. 'Remember her name because she's going to be a big star some day!'

I loved seeing all the different nationalities and cultures at the Games. Every culture was so different and colourful. Each night, New Zealand and Polynesian dancers would set up outside the dining room and start dancing and swaying to music. I thought the women were beautiful with their long hair, bikini tops and hula skirts. They also wore tropical flowers on their heads like crowns.

There was always something going on. If it wasn't music and dancing, then it was the Aussie athletes providing the entertainment. The Aussie team, particularly the boys, were pretty cheeky. They had a habit of starting up food fights after dinner. In the mornings I'd get up and see all this squashed, leftover food on the pathways.

I was running in the relay with three other girls: my two room-mates, plus Kerry Johnson. Kerry was Australia's number-one sprinter at the time and she'd been really sweet to me. She helped me at training and generally looked out for the 'baby' of the team.

One day I overheard some people talking in our unit. I recognised Kerry's voice straightaway. 'There's no way I'm letting Jane Flemming take Catherine's place!' she said.

My heart sank – they were thinking of dropping me from the relay team! Jane Flemming was a heptathlete and she'd already picked up her second gold medal at the Games. I was devastated.

Kerry stuck up for me. 'We've been practising as a team for weeks. Jane can't just come in at the last minute and disrupt everything. If Catherine doesn't run, then I won't run!'

I couldn't hear much after that, but thanks to Kerry the others backed down and I got to keep my place on the team.

When the race day arrived, I was feeling quite calm. The relay is a tricky event: each runner has to concentrate not only on running fast, but on passing the baton safely into the next girl's hands. We'd done enough practise to feel confident that we could pass the baton on smoothly.

'I think we'll win this today,' Kerry said as we walked out onto the track. I wished the other girls well, then took off my warm-up clothes and walked to my position. I was running third after Kathy, and I had to pass the baton to Kerry, who was running the final leg of the race.

I watched as the gun went off – *Bang!* – and the race started. Monique ran the first leg and passed the baton safely to Kathy. Before I knew it, Kathy was only sixty metres away from me. I'd been so focused on watching my team-mates, I had no idea what position we were in. All I knew was that Kathy, who's not a small girl, was moving towards me at full pelt like a freight train.

When she reached the sticky-tape marker on the track, it was my cue to take off. I started running as fast as I could. Kathy yelled out, 'Hand!' and I shot my left hand out behind me, just like we'd practised in training.

The baton change was perfect. (Phew!) Once I had a firm grip, I ran as fast as I could towards Kerry. Before I knew it, she was right in front of me. Her hand was outstretched, ready to sprint to the finish with the shiny, hollow baton.

Once she had it, she exploded away, and I slowed down just in time to watch her cross the finish line in first place. We'd won! I caught up with Monique and Kathy and together we ran over to join Kerry. We couldn't stop hugging each other and jumping for joy.

By the time they presented us with our medals the seriousness of the moment had hit me. When they played the national anthem, I sang the words as loud as I could – I was so proud and honoured.

Heaps of people came to the press conference

afterwards. Apparently someone had realised that I was first Aborigine to win a Commonwealth Games gold medal for track and field. Journalists kept asking me how that felt.

'Being Aboriginal means everything to me,' I said. 'So many of my friends have the talent, but lack the opportunity. I did this for all of us.'

Life is a funny thing at times. After my experience at the Commonwealth Games, I thought I'd be on top of the world for a very long time. But it didn't turn out that way.

A few days after I'd flown home to Queensland, my parents and I were at a neighbour's house, watching a replay of the closing ceremony on TV.

'That's you, Catherine!' Mum yelled when she spotted me on the screen. Mum and Bruce were so proud. They hadn't stopped asking me questions: Who did you meet? What was the village like? What did you eat?

I was still on an absolute high. The day before I'd been part of the Commonwealth Games celebrations in Brisbane. I was so happy it was like my feet didn't touch the ground.

I was just telling Mum about what it was like to do the victory lap when Bruce got a phone call. I didn't pay that much attention – I thought it was probably his work. But as soon as he hung up, I could tell something was wrong.

'Anne-Marie's dead,' he said.

In that moment, all the world's sunshine was taken away.

It took a couple of seconds for Mum to realise what she'd heard. Then she just fell apart. She cried out in pain and love. She couldn't believe that her oldest daughter was gone.

Bruce told us that Anne-Marie had died of an asthma attack. She was only twenty-four. I sat there in shock, feeling like my heart was breaking. How could one moment bring you so much joy and laughter, and the next cause you so much pain?

Anne-Marie's funeral was held in Rockhampton. I wanted to have my gold medal buried with her, but Mum talked me out of it.

'Ma, I want Anne-Marie to have it,' I said.

'No, Catherine,' she said. 'One day you'll want to show that medal to your grandchildren. That's what Anne-Marie would have wanted.'

We buried the flower posy from my medal ceremony with Anne-Marie instead. As I stood at the grave with my family, I suddenly knew what I had to do. I had to run for Anne-Marie. I promised myself that from that day onwards, every race I ran would be for her.

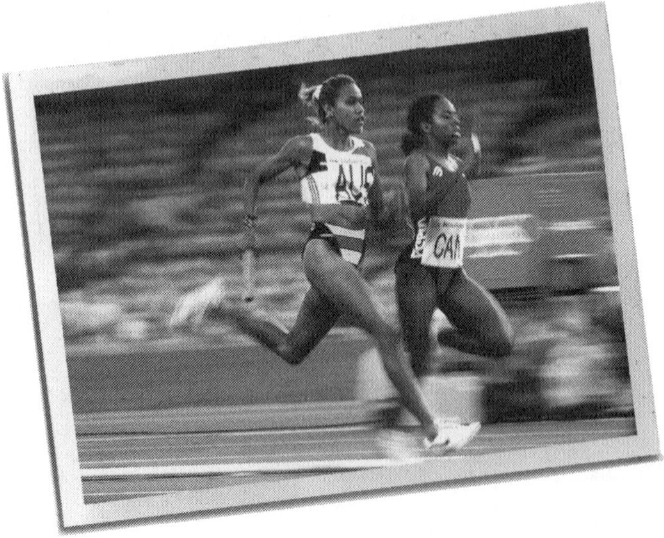
AUS
CAN

CHAPTER 8
First Olympics

By the time I was eighteen, I'd finished school and moved from sunny Queensland down to Melbourne in Victoria. Although I'd won a Commonwealth Games gold medal, I was still dreaming about the Olympics. But I didn't just want to compete in relays any more – I wanted to run in my *own* event.

My coach in Melbourne was a middle-aged man with thin, silvery hair called Peter Fortune. Fort was pretty calm and relaxed, which suited me. He'd coached other Australian champions and thought my fluid running style was best suited to the 400m event. I had run a few 400m races over the years, but I'd never really focused on it. The first time I'd raced that distance was when I was twelve. I ate a Mars Bar just before the start and all the way round I could feel it. I collapsed when I crossed the finished line and almost threw up.

Together Fort and I started training for the Barcelona Olympic trials. The day I heard I'd been selected, I was over the moon! I'd qualified to run in both the individual 400m sprint and the 400m relay. I couldn't help thinking back to the time when my old high school teacher Sess had told me I'd go to the Olympics one day.

The first thing I did when I got to Barcelona was call Mum. She'd been holidaying overseas for a few weeks and was staying with some friends in Israel.

'Hey, Ma,' I said. 'How are you doing?'

'I'm good, darling,' she said. 'My friends are taking really good care of me. Where are you?'

'I'm in the Olympic village, Ma. It's right by the ocean so it feels like a holiday resort. I start competing in a week or so. You'll be here in time, won't you?'

'Of course, I will,' Mum said. 'I wouldn't come this far only to miss my girl competing in her first Olympics!'

In the athletes' village I shared a room with long-distance walker Kerry Saxby. Our apartment was on the third floor and we had a TV room, a kitchen, a bathroom and one bedroom. The bedroom window had a view of the street. Every morning I got woken up when a noisy garbage truck came to collect the rubbish.

Just before I'd left Australia, one of my friends had given me an Aboriginal flag as a present, and I hung this on the bedroom wall for everyone to see. It made me feel so proud with its beautiful colours of black, red and gold.

Even though we had our own kitchen, Kerry and I ate most of our meals in the huge dining room. If the dining room at the Commonwealth Games had seemed big, this one was like a small town. The whole Olympic village was incredible – there were movie theatres, beauty salons, and even a games parlour. I was lucky I didn't get lost. Everywhere you went there was something or someone to look at – including athletes from every country in the world.

My races weren't on till the second week of the Games, so I had plenty of time to explore. I loved walking around Barcelona – the warm salty air reminded me of Queensland. Then there were the official events at the village. I sat in on a press conference with Michael Jordan and the pole vaulter Sergei Bubka. Everything felt like an adventure.

On opening ceremony night, I was in the front row of the Australian team. I entered the stadium to see bright lights and hear thousands of people cheering. You could feel the electricity in the air.

I knew our lap around the stadium would be something I'd want to remember forever. As we walked, I spotted the actress Phylicia Rashad in the crowd. It was such a thrill to see her in person – she played the mother character on one of my favourite TV shows, *The Cosby Show*. Just as we came to the end of our lap, the American basketball team entered the stadium. I couldn't believe I was seeing legends like Charles Barkley and Magic Johnson up close. Everyone – including me – thought they were so cool.

By the time the second week arrived, I was still feeling overawed. There are four stages in the 400m event: the first heat, the second heat, the semi-final and the final. As I walked onto the track for my first heat, I couldn't get over how many people were in the stands. This is it! I thought. My first race at the Olympics. I found my focus in time to run a good race – I was just beaten on the line to come second.

The next day, Mum arrived in the village. I was on a bus on the way to training when I saw her outside the Olympic stadium.

'Mum! Mum!' I screamed out the window. I was so happy to see her, I had tears in my eyes. That night Mum asked my manager if we were going to have a party after I'd won the gold medal. She was so used to me winning – she didn't see why the Olympics would be any different.

On the day of my second heat, I felt so relaxed I was almost in a dream world. When the gun went off, I wasn't ready and made a slow start. I picked up speed in the second half, but it was too late – I only managed to come fifth. The first four girls made it through to the semi-final. I was out of the race.

It was a huge blow, but when I saw Mum she just sat me down on her lap and hugged me. 'It's okay,' she said, stroking my hair. 'There'll be other Games.'

Together we watched the 400m final from the stands. A woman from France, Marie-José Pérec, ended up taking home the gold medal.

Our 400m relay team finished seventh in the final. It was another disappointment, but I didn't let it get me down for long. Now that I'd had my first taste of the Olympics, I knew that I'd be back. I wanted to be like Kieran Perkins and Marie-José Pérec, who'd both won gold medals at the Games. I was sure that winning was part of my destiny.

When I got home, I found a label and wrote down the number 48.60. Marie-José had run the 400m in a time of 48.82 seconds, so I figured 48.60 was my 'magic' number – the time I needed to run to win a gold medal at the Olympics.

As I stuck the label on the mirror beside my bed, I remembered the certificate I'd made when I was ten. I found another bit of paper and wrote out the same words: I AM THE WORLD'S GREATEST ATHLETE. I figured that if it had got me this far, maybe it could work again.

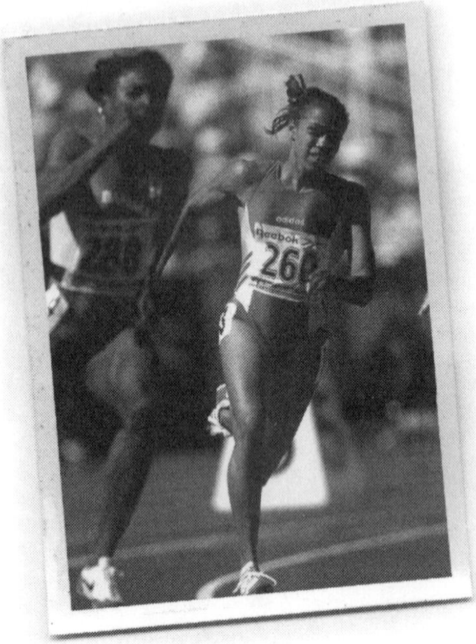
Reebok

CHAPTER 9
Two Gold

As I walked towards the departure gates at the airport, I looked back over my shoulder at Mum and Bruce. I was just about to board a plane to Europe and from there I'd fly to Canada to compete in the 1994 Commonwealth Games. Instead of waving, I held up two fingers.

'Two gold!' I called out.

My parents laughed and waved back at me.

I couldn't believe it! I'd just predicted I was going to win two gold medals. Why do I feel so confident? I wondered. Maybe it was just because I knew I'd been training hard and my health and fitness were good. It made me feel ready to take on the world.

This time when I got to the athletes' village, I wasn't as overwhelmed as I had been at my first Games in Auckland. It was a bit like: 'been there, done that!' Although I did think the city where the Games were being held – Victoria in Canada – was very pretty. It's really green and is surrounded by beautiful lakes. It made the atmosphere at the Games seem quite friendly and relaxed.

But I hadn't come to Canada to muck about. My aim was to win. Every time I stepped onto a track, my instincts were always the same – to beat the competition.

My desire to win wasn't just about me, though. I also wanted to represent my people, the Australian Aborigines. Being Aboriginal means so much to me – it gives me strength and makes me proud. Along with the memory of my sister, Anne-Marie, my Aboriginal ancestors inspire me to be all that I can be.

At my first Olympics in Barcelona, I had proudly displayed an Aboriginal flag in my room. This time I asked a friend to hold it up in the crowd when I raced. It made me feel good to see any Aussie flag, but when I saw the Aboriginal flag it meant something different. It reminded me who I was and where I'd come from.

As I walked to the blocks for the 400m final, I adjusted the black, red and gold scrunchie I wore in my hair. I was running in lane three and I knew the two girls I had to beat – Fatima Yusuf from Nigeria and Sandie Richards from Jamaica – were in lanes four and five.

The gun went off, and I went for it! I could tell that I was running well. I was in 'the zone'. Being in the zone is like having a force field over you – you don't necessarily hear or feel or even see what's all around you. During that race the only thing I was aware of was myself and my desire to win.

And I did!

I was so happy. I ran straight over to my friend and grabbed my Aboriginal flag. A woman I didn't know handed me an Australian flag so I draped both of them over my shoulders like a cape. I felt so strong and proud as I jogged my victory lap. I was halfway towards my goal of winning two gold medals at the Games.

That night I stayed in the village and celebrated with a few friends. I had a great night, but I couldn't party too hard because I still had to race in the 200m the following day.

The next morning, someone told me that Arthur Tunstall had been talking about me in the news. Arthur Tunstall was the Commonwealth Games Federation President so when he spoke, people listened. Basically, Mr Tunstall was upset that I'd done a victory lap with the Aboriginal flag. He said I wasn't allowed to do it again if I won the 200m.

That's crazy, I thought. I'm not breaking any of the rules!

As I made my way down to the warm-up track, I was suddenly surrounded by journalists. 'So, Cathy,' one of them called out, 'what's your reaction to the way Arthur Tunstall has been criticising you?'

I started to open my mouth to speak when another journalist shoved a microphone in my face.

'Cathy! If you win the two hundred metres, will you carry both flags in your victory lap again?'

I looked at the journalist and smiled. 'Yeah, I guess so,' I said, and kept walking.

I didn't understand why they were making such a fuss. It was just a flag! But I couldn't let it distract me – I had to stay focused on my running. Luckily, later that morning I received the blessing of the Athletics Australia president, Neil King, to carry *both* my Aboriginal flag and the Aussie flag if I won the 200m.

There was so much talk of me winning that race, but it still wasn't a guarantee. Unlike the 400m race, I wasn't the favourite for the 200m. The fastest 200m runner was a woman from Nigeria called Mary Onyali.

Just before the race, Fort told me not to worry if I was behind at the start. 'Even if it doesn't feel like it, you can still win,' he said.

I took my position in lane three. Just as Fort had predicted, I was slow going out. C'mon, Freeman, I thought, you can still do this. With eighty metres to go, I had a surge of energy. I was flying, soaring on the air just above the track. In the last three metres I passed Mary Onyali to cross the finish line first.

Wow! I'd done it again!

Without hesitating, I grabbed both the Aboriginal and the Australian flag and did another victory lap. I hoped that people in the crowd would understand that while I was proud to represent Australia, I was just as proud to represent Indigenous Australia. We're all different, I felt like saying, but we all belong to the same country.

By carrying both flags, I wasn't trying to divide a nation — I was trying to display my pride in who I was and where I'd come from. I wanted other Aboriginal kids to see me and think, If she can do it, why can't I do it? A few weeks later, I read a survey in the paper that said the majority of Aussies thought I'd done the right thing.

The rest of the Games were a bit of a blur. Back in the athletes' village I received thousands of letters and faxes from all over Australia. People opened their hearts to me, saying how happy and delighted they were. One woman even wrote that when she saw me run around with the flag, she felt that for the first time in her life it was worth being Aboriginal. As I read the letter my eyes filled with tears.

When I got back home to Melbourne, lots of things had changed. Newspaper and TV stations called non-stop for interviews. People recognised me on the street. It was as if I wasn't Catherine any more, I was 'Cathy Freeman – gold medal winner'.

My life was stuck in fast forward for weeks. I was invited to parties, lunches, parades and gala events. I even had afternoon tea with the Prime Minister at the time, Paul Keating. It seemed that everyone in Australia wanted to meet me. To be honest, it was a little weird!

I was so tired at the end of every day. When the time came to get back to training and a simpler lifestyle, I was relieved. The attention had been nice for a while, but I didn't want to lose sight of my dream. The most important thing was having time to do what I loved the most – to run.

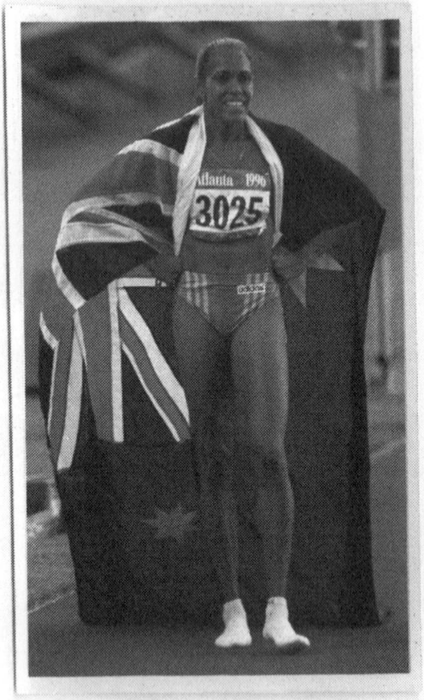
1996
3025

CHAPTER 10
Number Two

By the time I was twenty-two, I was ranked Number Two in the world in the women's 400m. Marie-José Pérec, the winner of the gold medal at the Barcelona Olympics, was Number One.

Three years after Barcelona, Marie-José and I raced against each other at a competition in Monte Carlo. Marie-José hadn't lost a 400m race in over five years.

Okay, Freeman, I told myself as I walked to the starting blocks, you can do this.

The gun fired and we were off. Marie-José's usual style was to run hard from the start and set up such a gap that it was impossible to beat her. This time it was different – I was right next to her, matching her stride for stride. With a hundred and fifty metres to go, I had a surge of energy. I ran past her and crossed the finish line in first place.

I couldn't believe it! Marie-José was the world's best and I had beaten her! Now that I had done it once, I was convinced I could do it again.

The next time we competed against each other was at the 1995 World Championships in Sweden. I went into the race full of confidence. When my coach Fort tried to talk to me about my race plan, I didn't really listen. What's the point? I thought. I already know how to beat Marie-José!

As we walked onto the track I spotted a friend in the crowd holding up my Aboriginal flag. Instead of thinking about the race, I started thinking about how I would feel once I was the world champion.

The announcement came to take our positions

on the blocks when all of a sudden it hit me: I was just about to run one of the biggest races in my career. I was terrified!

'On your marks,' the starter said.

This is it, I thought. The starter gun went off, and I bolted.

I was flying around the track. I was going to be the next world champion! As we ran into the last hundred metres, I was dead level with Marie-José. *Okay, it's time to show her what you can do. Go girl!*

Then with eighty metres left to go, something happened. I was starting to slow down. No, I thought. Please, no!

I had 'hit the wall'. This is what we call it when athletes run out of energy. It feels like you're running in slow motion. As I ran the last sixty metres, my legs and arms felt like cement. I could only watch as Marie-José moved further and further ahead. Then another two athletes ran past me. I wasn't even going to get a medal.

I was so angry with myself. I could have won, or at least come second, but I'd stuffed up completely. The race had been a disaster.

As disappointed as I was, I'd just learnt a crucial lesson: in racing, you can't get ahead of yourself. I'd wanted to win so badly that I'd lost my focus. Instead of concentrating on things I could control, like my breathing and my race plan, I'd only thought about winning. Now I knew that if I wanted to do my best, I had to stay focused.

I took this lesson to heart. The Atlanta Olympics were only a year away and I wanted to be ready. I dedicated myself to training like never before. If Fort told me to do fifty sit-ups, I would do sixty. If training started at 8 a.m, I'd be there at 7.45 a.m. I remembered the advice of my old coach Mike: if you want to achieve anything great, you had to work hard. I knew there was no other way.

When I arrived in Atlanta, I was in the best shape of my life. Unlike the Barcelona Olympics, this time I wasn't competing as an inexperienced teenager, I was a world-class athlete. I was the fastest female 400m runner in Australia, and everyone expected me to at least make it into the final. But I didn't let the pressure get to me. I was just there to do what I was born to do: to run and run fast.

I'd already worked out a race plan with my manager Nick. We'd talked about it one afternoon in a café over hot chocolates. Nick told me he'd written out a six-point race plan for me.

'I think that's too long,' I said. 'It will be too hard to remember. How about we use an acronym instead?' An acronym is a word where every letter stands for something else.

Nick came up with the word FLAG. He wrote it down for me on the back of the café receipt.

'**F** stands for *Fly*,' he said. 'When the race starts, you *fly* out of the blocks. **L** is for *Leg speed* as you run the first hundred metres. **A** is for *Attack* – this is the time when you should overtake anyone in front of you. And **G** is for *Go!* when you run at top speed all the way to the finish line.'

It sounded good to me. 'So how do you think I'll go?' I asked.

'I think if you run your best you'll come first or second,' Nick said.

'I think I'll come second,' I said quickly.

There are times when you say something and afterwards you're not really sure why you said it.

93

Second! Why hadn't I said first? Maybe I was trying to make sure my expectations weren't too high.

On the night of the final, I put the receipt with the word FLAG on the back in my race bag. I also packed my spiked running shoes. I'd been planning to wear a special pair with the Aboriginal flag on the sides, but when I tried them on, they hurt my toes. My regular spikes would have to do.

As we drove to the track, I told myself that this was going to be just like a rollercoaster ride: exciting, fun and scary all at the same time. It was my way of trying to distract myself from how nervous I was.

My main rival was Marie-José. Although I'd beaten her once, she'd proved time and time again that she was the best. She was so strong, and we had completely different styles. She always ran full-pelt at the start of a race, getting such a good lead on her competition that no one could beat her. I had a habit of cruising and only doing any real 'work' in the last hundred metres or so. I knew if I wanted to beat Marie-José again, I'd have to stay with her right from the start.

As I entered the stadium with the other athletes,

it was like I'd been hypnotised. I was so focused, I didn't notice what was going on around me. I was definitely in the zone. Two of my friends, Tiff and Peta, were both sitting near the entrance, screaming my name out at the top of their lungs. I didn't hear them even though they were less than twenty metres away!

I stripped off my leggings, adjusted the number on my top and began kicking nervously at the track. I was running in lane four and Marie-José was in lane three. Remember the plan, I thought.

When the starter gun went off, I flew out of the blocks and ran the second hundred metres at a nice cruising speed. As we came to the 200m mark, I realised Marie-José still hadn't passed me. Yes! The first part of the plan had gone perfectly.

At that moment, Marie-José made her move. Time for 'A' – *Attack*.

We were coming to the final straight. In a 400m race, it's the last hundred metres that really count. At that point, you're so tired you need every scrap of energy in your body, heart and soul to get you across the line in first place.

With about seventy metres to go, Marie-José passed me. A thought flashed through my mind: *I've got the silver*. But I still gave it everything and sped up until we were neck and neck. For what felt like forever I was at her elbow. She was so tall and her stride was so long, but I was still right with her. Then with ten metres to go, I felt myself weaken. No, I thought, she's too strong. I knew it was over and watched as Marie-José won by three metres.

As I crossed the finish line, I clapped my hands above my head, congratulating myself on a good race. Then I looked up at the clock. My time was 48.63 seconds. I couldn't believe it! That was almost the same as my magic number: the one I had stuck on my mirror at home.

I looked up and saw Australian flags flying in the crowd. For the first time, I realised people were cheering for me. My head was spinning trying to take it all in. I was an Olympic silver medallist!

As I got ready for the medal ceremony, I realised I'd forgotten to pack my tracksuit. The team doctor found out and ran around like crazy trying to get one for me. In the end I had to borrow Debbie Flintoff-

King's trackpants and another athlete's top. I watched as Marie-José took out a beauty kit and started putting on make-up. She'd done some modelling in Paris and obviously knew what she was doing.

'Hey, Marie,' I said, 'can I use some of that?'

'Sure.' She smiled and helped me put on lipstick and mascara. It was fun. Marie-José had never been that friendly towards me before so I was touched. For a moment it felt like we weren't rivals, we were just two girls getting ready to head out for a party.

When I stepped onto the dais to get my silver medal, I couldn't stop smiling and waving at the crowd. Even though I hadn't won, I still felt like a champion.

But later that night, I started to wonder if maybe I'd jinxed myself into getting the silver. Why had I told my manager I'd come second instead of first? Had I thought I couldn't beat Marie-José again?

The more I thought about it, the more it made sense: I hadn't won because I hadn't backed myself one hundred percent. Something in me had been satisfied with coming second. Next time, I decided, I'm going for gold!

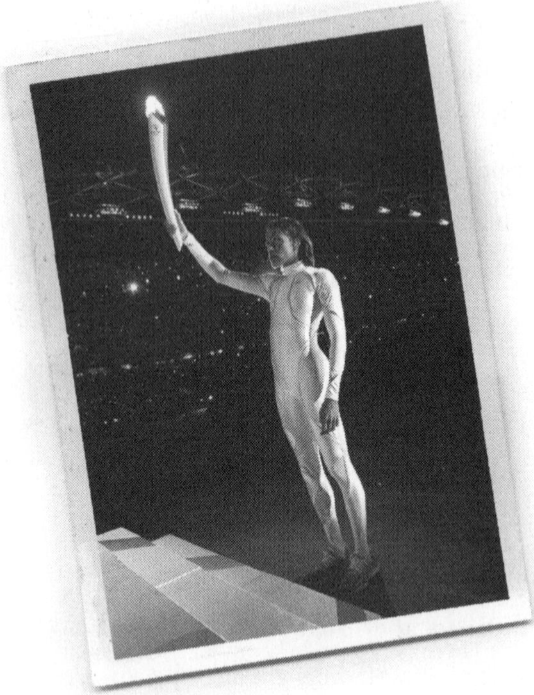

CHAPTER 11
The Big Secret

'And the winner is... Sydney!'

I heard the announcement and started jumping up and down in my lounge room. I had stayed up late to find out which city would be chosen to host the Olympic Games in the year 2000. And Sydney had won!

By that time I'd already been in two Olympics, but I knew it would be different competing in

Australia. Now my whole family could come and watch me at the Games.

It was more incentive than ever to make it into the team. There was going to be a lot of pressure on me, running in my home country, but I knew I couldn't let it distract me. My goal was to win an Olympic gold medal, and I had to do everything in my power to make that goal happen.

Twice a day, every day, I was either running on the track, or at the gym, or bounding up hills, or on my carpet doing weights. I made sure I got eight hours of sleep every night, and during the week I had regular massage treatments. If I went out on the weekend, I never wore shoes with high heels because they did too much damage to my feet.

My diet was also pretty strict. It included lots of fresh fruit and vegetables, which I'd steam or grill, or eat raw. I only ate red meat about once a week; mostly I just had fish or chicken. Fried food and fast food was out. But I did like to snack. Some of my favourite snacks were almonds, low-fat rice pudding, and even baby food.

Everything I did was geared towards winning. My

days were structured with military-style discipline, but I also took some time out to be silly and have a bit of fun. It was really important for me to be able to relax in the lead-up to the Games. Fort and I started referring to the Sydney Olympics as 'just another athletics carnival'. It helped to take some of the pressure off and always made me laugh.

Five months before the opening ceremony I had dinner with John Coates, the boss of the Australian Olympic Committee. I'd known him for a few years and figured he was just checking in to see how things were going. But then he told me the real reason for the dinner.

'Cathy, would you please do us the honour of lighting the cauldron at the Sydney Olympics?' he said.

John's question came as a complete surprise. I'd had no idea the committee were thinking of asking me. I knew it was a huge honour.

'Yes, yes, yes!' I said, nearly jumping out of my chair. 'Of course I will!'

John was smiling. 'But you can't tell anyone,' he said. 'Not a soul. It's a big secret.'

John told me that besides the president of the International Olympic Committee and a few other people, nobody is allowed to know who's going to light the cauldron before opening night. I'm not sure how this tradition came about, but I wasn't about to break it by telling anybody – not even my mum!

'Hey, Catherine!' Steve Moneghetti, the famous marathon runner, was trying to get my attention. 'My bet is on you!'

I just smiled and kept quiet. It was opening ceremony night and I was waiting with the rest of the Australian team for our turn to march into the Olympic stadium. For the last hour everyone had been trying to guess who would light the cauldron. I hadn't said a word.

Finally we got the call to start moving towards the entrance. As walked through the stadium tunnels, I couldn't see the people in the crowd, but I could certainly feel them. The thick concrete slabs above our heads were vibrating so much it was as if the walls were talking.

We stepped out into the bright lights and there

was a jet-engine roar from the crowd. The place was going off! Everyone was so proud to be Australian. As soon as they saw us walking towards them they'd start screaming or jumping up and down. I'd never experienced anything like it.

I looked over at my team-mate Alison Inverarity and her face was streaked with tears. I was too excited to cry. I tried to find someone I knew in the crowd, but gave up after only a few minutes. Unless you've arranged something with your friends and family beforehand, it's almost impossible. But there were plenty of other things to look at. And I knew in the back of my mind that I still had a very important job to do...

The lights in the stadium darkened and a spotlight beamed onto centre stage. I stood with the rest of the Aussie team as Olivia Newton-John and John Farnham started singing 'Dare to Dream'. About halfway through the performance, someone tapped me on the shoulder. It was time to start getting ready. As I moved away from the others, I could hear their whispers: 'See, I *knew* it would be Cathy Freeman lighting the cauldron!'

I was taken to one of the rooms underneath the stadium. I quickly changed out of my opening ceremony uniform into a special bodysuit made of white-and-turquoise spandex. The spandex material shimmered in the light, and I had a matching pair of Nike running shoes to wear. I also had to get 'wired up', which means I had to wear an earpiece so I could hear instructions from the creative director. But the earpiece wasn't working properly – instead of hearing the director's voice, all I could hear was static.

'Can you hear the director now, Cathy?' one of the assistants said.

I shook my head. 'Nope. Sorry!'

'Maybe you should turn the volume up. Do you know how?'

'Ahh...' I searched for a volume button on the control box. 'Is it here?'

'Yeah, that's it.'

The next thing I knew, I was surrounded by at least six people who were all doing their 'bit' to make the earpiece work. It felt like I was being poked and prodded by a mini army, but I could see how worried and concerned they were. Everyone was talking at once, giving me directions and fiddling with the controls.

'Is it working now, Cathy?' someone asked.

'No.' I shook my head again. 'All I can hear is static.'

By this time everyone was panicking. They decided to replace my whole earpiece, but the new one wasn't working either!

Someone pulled me aside. 'Cathy, we can't get the earpiece to work. You'll just have to do everything you did in the rehearsal, but without instructions from the creative director. Will that be okay?'

I nodded. I just wanted to get it all over and done with. I knew that once I got through tonight, I'd be one step closer to racing. But then I heard a voice in my ear. The earpiece was working!

'Yeah! I've got it now!' I said in relief.

I was led out to the bottom of the main stairs leading up to the cauldron, where I'd receive the Olympic torch from Debbie Flintoff-King. As I waited, I ran through in my mind what I had to do: take the flame from Debbie, run up the stairs, and set the cauldron alight. Simple! Sure, there were lots of technicalities behind the scenes, but as long as I did what I'd done in rehearsals, I knew I'd be okay. It wasn't rocket science – well, my bit wasn't, anyway.

I was really focused on what I had to do, so I didn't hear much of the crowd, but I did hear my name being announced over the loudspeaker. They'd said it too early! Debbie was still about fifty metres away. She jogged the last bit and handed the torch to me. 'Enjoy it, it's great,' she whispered in my ear.

The first thing I had to do was jog up five flights of stairs to an artificial pond. The stairs were covered in flowing water. All I could think was: Don't trip and fall! The soles of my Nikes weren't made for jogging on slippery surfaces, but it was too late to worry about that now. I took a deep breath and started the climb.

When I got to the top, I paused to catch my breath. I'd made it! My next step was a bit shaky, but I had a huge grin on my face as I walked to the middle of the pond. I turned around to salute the crowd and was nearly blinded by light as flashes of thousands of cameras around the stadium went off.

Just like I'd practised, I leant over to light the cauldron, which was shaped like a flying saucer. It became a ring of fire.

I stood in the middle of the pond, under a circular waterfall, while the flying-saucer cauldron rose up around me. It must have looked pretty spectacular, but I was getting soaked – and the water was freezing! Now I just had to wait for a few minutes while the cauldron went all the way to the top and I could walk back down the stairs.

'We've got a slight technical hitch, Cathy,' came a voice in my ear. 'Nothing that can't be fixed.'

Uh oh! I thought. What's going on?

The cauldron had got stuck on its way to the top. The big steel 'beast' was refusing to move and just stopped and bounced a couple of times. The voice in my earpiece told me to salute the crowd with the torch, which I did. It was hauntingly quiet. All I could see was one hundred and ten thousand people with their fluorescent lights calmly swaying in the night. It's only when I think about it now that I realise how many millions of people around the world were watching me at that point.

'Okay, Cathy,' said the voice in my ear, 'one last wave and you can go down.' Phew! They'd got the cauldron working again.

At the bottom of the stairs I was joined by Australian sporting legends Dawn Fraser, Debbie Flintoff-King, Raelene Boyle, Shane Gould, Shirley Strickland and Betty Cuthbert. Dawn noticed that I was shivering and grabbed a jacket to wrap around my shoulders. Together we stood and watched the cauldron flames.

By the time I got back to my hotel later that night I was exhausted. The opening ceremony had been magical, but now that it was over part of me was relieved that I could concentrate on my real reason for being at the Olympics. In a little over a week I would run the biggest race of my entire life.

There were only ten more sleeps to go.

CHAPTER 12
Dreams Come True

It was 9 a.m. and I was lying in bed, staring at the wall. My big day had come: the 400m Olympic final. This was the day I'd been thinking and dreaming about since I was a little girl, the day I was going to win an Olympic gold medal.

Earlier in the week I had found out that Marie-José Pérec wasn't going to compete. I'd run in to Fort on my way to get a massage in the Olympic village when he told me the news. 'Have you heard?' he said.

'Heard what?'

'Pérec's gone. She flew out of Sydney early this morning.'

'No way,' I said. Fort told me there was talk that she'd had some kind of breakdown. I hoped she was okay. Even though we were rivals, I really liked Marie-José. She was the same age as Anne-Marie would have been.

I was also really disappointed. I wanted my chance to compete against her in another Olympic final. Races were always more exciting when Marie-José was in them – she brought my running to another level.

To get into the final, I'd had to run in three preliminary races: two heats and a semi-final. I won them all comfortably – although each race had been different.

In my first heat, there were so many moths flying around, I had to wave them away from my face. A few of them even got caught and squashed under my heavy steel starter-block.

Here I am training in the sandhills in South Stradbroke Island, Queensland, in 1999. I look serious — I must be training hard!

The chance to train on the beach always made me happy. Here I am flying in 1999.

This is me at the national championships in Sydney in 2000. I'm always happy to sign stuff for kids — even their running shoes!

This was a really proud moment for me lighting the cauldron at the 2000 Sydney Olympic Games. But I still had to race... and win!

Of course! The opening ceremony at the Sydney 2000 Olympics. I'm freezing here — but, hey, don't I look good!

And I'm off! This was my first heat for the 400m race at the Sydney 2000 Olympic Games.

Lucky I don't mind running in the rain — it was pouring when we ran the 400m semi-final.

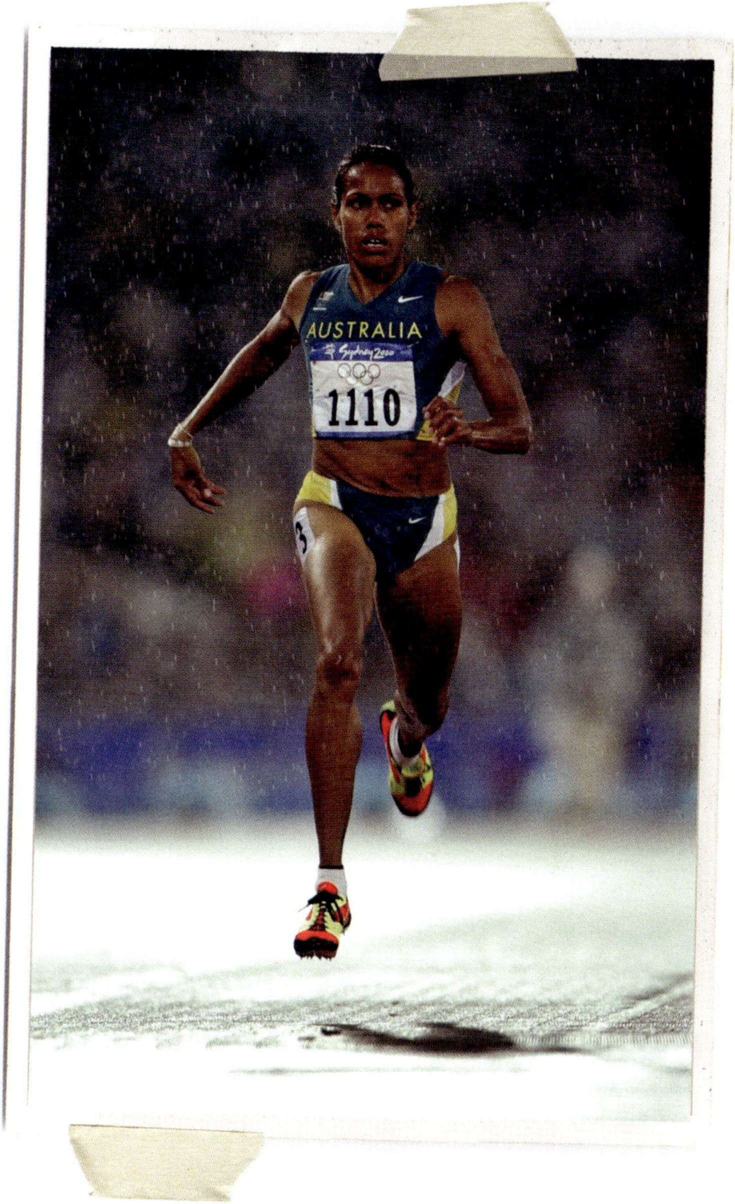
AUSTRALIA
Sydney 2000
1110

Can you tell I'm ready to win?
Here I am in the 400m final at the
Sydney 2000 Olympics.

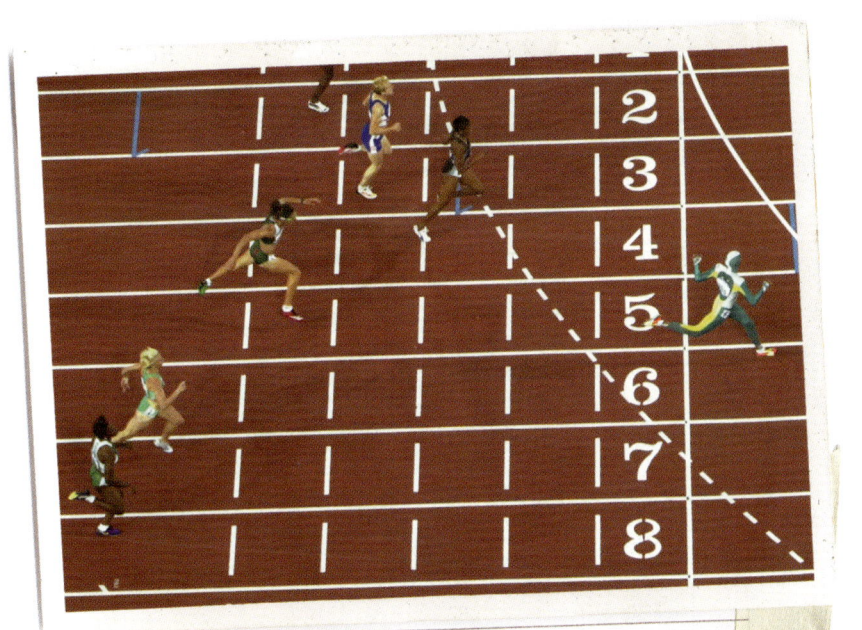

I love that winning feeling, especially when it happens at home in Australia.

How big is my smile! →

Look! There's my mum and my brother Garth in the crowd!

Finally, after 17 years I've done it.
And I'm still smiling!

I'll never, ever forget this moment.
It's awesome to make people feel so happy,
especially when they're your family.

Mum and me in 2001.
I couldn't have asked for
a better Mum.

I adore my step-dad, Bruce. I call him 'Blue Eyes.'

This is one of my favourite shots of my parents taken in 2002. They look so happy together at this party.

At one time I owned three cats — Billy
(the black one), Jazz (black and white),
and the fluffy white one is Nashi.
Luckily they all got on!

This is Ben and me. Isn't he gorgeous?
I'd go horse riding every day if I could.

I tell kids all the time that if I can do it, they can do it, too!

In my second heat, something happened that had never happened to me before. As I was running around the last bend, I glanced up into the crowd and wondered if Dad was watching me.

My dad had died a few years before, and I still felt sad whenever I thought about it. Even though I didn't get to spend much time with him while I was growing up, he's always had a special place in my heart. Just before he died I'd written him a letter saying that I would always love him and always be his baby girl. As I ran across the finish line in that heat, I hoped that wherever Dad was, he was proud of me.

On the day of the semi-final it was raining. Luckily I love running in the rain so it didn't bother me. My old coach, Mike, used to tell us: 'You've got to train no matter what the weather is.' He'd have us out there, running through slush and puddles, while everyone else was rugged up inside. As I watched the rain pelting down I knew I owed Mike a lot.

Now the race I'd been waiting for was only hours away. I hoped that all my training – every minute and second of it – was going to count. The race wasn't on till 9.40 p.m, which I guess is quite late, but I wouldn't have cared if it was at three in the morning. I was in the Olympic 400m women's final and I was going to win. Nothing was going to stop me!

I got up and ate my usual breakfast: cereal with honey, hot water, milk and a piece of fruit. Afterwards I chilled out in the apartment where I was staying. I read magazines, chatted, watched DVDs and played board games. Nothing out of the ordinary happened, but that was exactly how I wanted it.

The day seemed to fly and before I knew it I was standing in my bedroom, getting my bag ready to take to the track. I packed my racing number (1110), my spiked shoes and my favourite towel to sit and stretch on. Then I got out my swift suit. Nike had made me a special bodysuit that was designed to increase my speed by helping me slice through the air. I knew the suit would attract attention, which normally I wouldn't like, but I figured in an Olympic final everyone would be looking at me anyway. All I was concerned about was winning – I could have been wearing a hippopotamus suit for all I cared.

I took my time getting into the suit, making sure it felt comfortable. I'd already worn it a few times so I could get used to it. Getting the suit on is a bit different to putting on a leotard – it's much more fiddly. There's more material to pull up over your body and it clings to your skin like gladwrap.

On the way to the warm-up track I was very quiet. My training partner was chatting to me, but I didn't take in a word he said. I was already in my own world.

My warm-up was no different to any other warm-up I'd ever done – except that I'd waited a lifetime for this one. Everyone in my 'team' – my coach, my training partner and my masseuse – seemed to be in tune with me. Even Marie-José Pérec's coach came over and gave me a big hug.

'You can do it, girl,' he said.

You bet I can! I thought.

When I heard the final call for athletes, I felt a tiny doubt creep in. I beckoned Fort over.

'Will people still love me if I lose?' I asked.

Fort smiled. 'Of course they will,' he said. 'But you won't lose!'

I gave him a hug and walked to the room where we had to wait to be called out to the main track. For some athletes, the loneliness you feel as you walk away from your team can be really frightening and overwhelming. It can literally either make or break you. Luckily for me, those minutes before a race make me come to life. I have the ability to make myself feel strong and powerful and completely in control – even when my guts are churning, and my heart is beating wildly, and my legs feel like jelly. I knew I could win; now I just wanted to get out there and do it.

As we walked into the stadium, all I could focus on was my lane. My heart was pumping wildly – it felt like there was electricity flowing through my veins. I took a deep breath. I was ready.

I slipped off my tracksuit bottoms and long-sleeved T-shirt to reveal my swift suit. Then I set up my starting block so I could practise doing some starts. I was feeling strong, determined and fierce. As my name was called out, I clapped my hands above my head a couple of times. My lips felt dry so I licked them and told myself to breathe. A whistle sounded and I moved with the other athletes to the blocks. I got my feet into position and put my hands exactly on the starting line. Then I stared down the track and waited for the gun.

'On your marks, set...'

Bang!

The sound of the gun blasted through me and I took off. As I ran into the first bend, I took a deep breath and licked my lips again. My heart rate was going crazy. I had to remember to control my breathing otherwise I would run out of steam. I had waited a long time to win an Olympic gold medal, and I wasn't interested in waiting another four years for my next shot.

As I ran, I knew there was no way the others could beat me – not unless they'd taken some magic potion or something. I was just too strong. But I was still running a very cautious race. I was sticking to my race plan and not going any faster than I needed to. I wanted this victory more than I'd ever wanted anything in my whole life so there was a danger that I could lose control. When that happens, sometimes you don't have enough strength left, physically and emotionally, to come home and be first across the line.

At the 300m mark, I was still fairly even with the other seven girls. Time to make a move! I waited until we got to the home straight and then I surged ahead. When I came round the last bend and saw the finish line, I could smell victory. My body and muscles and heart felt so strong – it was like I could move mountains.

In the last sixty metres of the race, I felt the noise of the crowd for the first time. Their cheers had a strange effect on me – it was like I was being lifted up and carried towards the finish line. I could feel all this energy around me – the energy of my beloved family and my ancestors, and the energy of Australians everywhere who loved me and wanted me to win. I floated across the finish line five metres in front of anyone else.

I did it!

The wonderful, familiar feeling of winning washed over me. But this time it was different. I had just made a dream come true, one I'd had since I was ten years old. It was so unreal. I couldn't take in what I'd actually done. I'd waited so long for this moment and now it had been and gone.

I felt an overwhelming sense of relief. Not physical exhaustion, just sheer relief that all my longing, yearning, waiting and hard work had finally paid off. For the first time I became aware of where I was – standing in front of a crowd of one hundred and ten thousand people who'd all been expecting me to win. The noise was unbelievable!

All of a sudden I needed to sit down and take off my shoes. I wanted to feel the air between my toes. My friend and training partner, Donna Fraser, came and crouched next to me. I could see her lips moving, but I couldn't hear a word she was saying over the roar of the crowd.

I've always been shy about doing victory laps, but after I'd been hugged and kissed by the other competitors, I made my way over to my race planner, Maurie. 'Should I do a lap?' I asked.

He nodded and said, 'Yes, go around.' It was only then that I let myself really smile.

Off I went, jogging around the track. People had thrown Australian and Aboriginal flags on the ground and I picked up one of each and tied them around my neck.

'Yeeeeeeaaaaaahhhh!' I yelled.

The crowd was going wild. There were camera people and photographers everywhere and one of them tripped over, landing flat on his bum. 'Are you all right, mate?' I asked.

The Vanessa Amorosi song 'Absolutely Everybody' was playing and I skipped along, waving both flags madly. I loved it. As I jogged around the home straight, I felt my eyes drawn towards a certain spot in the crowd. And then I saw them – my family! It was a miracle that I'd been able to see them amongst all the thousands of people in the stands. It was as if fate knew that I needed to share this moment with them.

I saw my big brother, Gavin, waving and calling out to me. Mum and Garth were trying to climb over the railing so they could hug me. Norm and my nephew Gavin were yelling, 'One! One! One!' And Bruce's big blue eyes were sparkling. I'd never seen him look so happy.

When I finished my victory lap, a group of

reporters were waiting to talk to me. 'So, Cathy,' said Ernie Dingo, an Aboriginal TV presenter, 'if you could say something to the children of Australia right now, what would it be?'

I looked at him with a big smile on my face and answered from the heart. 'I'd tell them that dreams do come true!'

I was having such a terrific night, but it wasn't over yet. I still had to do a warm-down, meet up with my family, do a drugs test, talk at a press conference and go to the medal ceremony. I found my sports bag and started filling out a drug-testing form. I was always happy to fill out this form, because I would never use drugs. My dream was to the best runner I could be, not the best-runner-on-drugs I could be.

I saw my family again just before the medal ceremony. They were waiting for me in one of the rooms underneath the stadium. It was great to hug and kiss my parents, my brothers and my nephew when we all had so much joy in our hearts. Bruce had the biggest smile on his face. I knew that if it wasn't for him meeting my mum all those years ago, there was no way I'd be an Olympic champion.

The crowd let out a hugh cheer when we walked out to get our medals. I couldn't stop waving and jumping up and down. One of the International Olympic Committee Members, Kevan Gosper, was laughing as he hung the heavy gold medal around my neck. I held it up and turned around on the dais so the whole crowd could see. Then I raised my arms to the sky and it felt like the sun was shining out of my chest. I was a giant who had conquered the world.

On the way out of the stadium, I spotted my family in the crowd again. I wished that Anne-Marie and Dad could have been there with them. I'd been given a bouquet of flowers on the dais which I handed straight to Mum. She deserved so much more than those flowers, but at least it was a small way of saying thank you.

I still hadn't warmed down properly, so every chance I got, I jogged and stretched as much as I could. I didn't want to get injured, which is what can happen if you don't warm down after a big race.

There was so much going on, I didn't get home until around two o'clock in the morning. My family were waiting for me in the apartment. I was glad it was just us – as usual, I didn't want to make a big fuss. I'd won an Olympic gold medal, but the best thing about it was sharing it with my family.

Everyone was still trying to take it in.

'I can't believe it,' Norman said, over and over.

Bruce kept looking at me and shaking his head. 'It only took seventeen years,' he said.

It was so great just laughing and hanging out together. After a while, my parents had to get back to their friends' house where they were staying. Not surprisingly, my brothers decided to go out and hit the town.

After they left I had a shower and went to bed with a blissful, heavenly feeling: the satisfaction of having won that beautiful gold medal was forever imprinted on my heart.

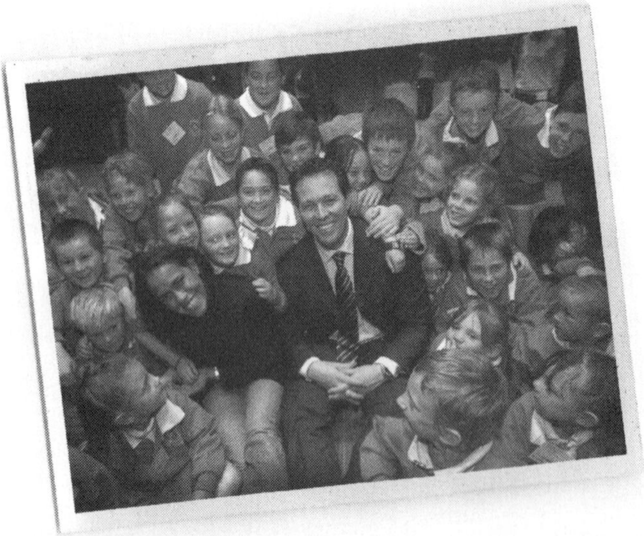

CHAPTER 13
After Gold

Life doesn't stop after you win a gold medal. When I woke up the morning after my race I was still buzzing with happiness. But part of me was thinking, 'What now?' For seventeen years I'd had a dream. Now my dream had come true. Where did I go from here?

I knew there was one thing I had to do. A few weeks after the Games, I made a special trip up north to visit Anne-Marie's grave. Every time things had got tough in the past ten years, I'd thought of my sister. She had been my guardian angel.

'I did it for you, Anne-Marie,' I whispered as I placed some flowers on her headstone.

I also went to visit my hometown of Mackay. I had barely got off the plane when I heard a little girl yell, 'Auntie Catherine! Auntie Catherine!' It was my niece Astrid. She came running up to me and jumped into my arms. All the family had come along. There were also about a thousand people lining the main street, and balloons and streamers everywhere. I waved to everyone and stopped to say a few words. 'I'm so proud of where I've come from,' I told them. 'It wasn't just me who won the gold medal, it was all of us.'

It wasn't until moments like this that I realised how many people had been hoping I'd win that 400m race. In the lead-up to the Sydney Olympic Games, I'd stopped reading the newspapers and watching TV. I didn't want to know what people were saying about me so I wouldn't get offended or feel any extra pressure. Now people would stop me to tell me how much my race meant to them.

A breakfast-show host in America even said, 'Cathy, your race struck a chord throughout the world.'

It's an amazing thing to have your dreams come true. But in another way it's scary – like stepping out of a warm, safe house into the wilderness. You have to find new dreams and new mountains to climb. In life, there's no finish line.

Three years after the Sydney Olympics, I retired from running. After all those years of training and competing, it was a really hard thing to do. Running was what I had always done and it was what I was best at. But it also takes total commitment and I knew that my heart just wasn't in it any more. It was time to find a new passion.

Now I look at the rest of my life as the next big adventure. I never wanted to become famous, but one of the great things about being 'Cathy Freeman' is that you get to help people. One way I can do that is by visiting schools and speaking to Aboriginal kids. When I was growing up I had amazing support from my parents, coaches and teachers, but not everyone has the same opportunities. That's one of the reasons

I got involved with an organisation called Inspire. It's a non-profit organisation that aims to help young people get through tough times. I tell kids that even sporting champions have bad days. We make mistakes just like everyone else.

'You're not alone,' I say, 'so please be kind to yourself and never lose sight of your dreams.'

One of the dreams I have for the future is to raise a family of my own. Family has always been important to me. When I ran, I didn't just run for me – I ran for Mum and Bruce, for all my brothers and my relatives, for my late nanna and my dad and Anne-Marie. They made me who I am. I hope I can give my own family as much love and support one day. I want to be the kind of person that my grandkids and their friends would want to hang out with.

So that's my story. I hope you've enjoyed it and that it's inspired you to live your own dreams. Remember to follow your heart. Live honestly, love learning, laugh loudly and you can't go wrong.

Dreams do come true!

Cathy Freeman's Ten Hot Tips

> ①
> Don't forget that there's always something about you that people really love.

It can sometimes be easy to forget what it is about yourself that makes you so very special, unique and totally loveable, but never ever forget that we are all meant to be different and no two people are the same.

> ②
> It's okay to be a little scared and frightened, because at times everybody else is feeling the same way.

Everybody feels scared and lonely sometimes. It's all right. Fear is something we have to feel every now and again so that we can learn new things about ourselves, that's all!

> ③
> Know that there is always somebody right near you who wants you to tell them exactly how you feel.

Telling somebody else about yourself is always a great thing, and sharing our feelings and thoughts and listening to other people is something we should all do.

> ④
> Always try your hardest to be kind and well-mannered to others.

When you are kind to people, they are kind to you. Nice things happen to nice people!

> ⑤
> Respect your elders.

Older people usually know more than younger people – they've lived for longer! They deserve to be listened to and cared for.

> ⑥
> Remember that the one precious thing you really do own is your health.

If you're not healthy, then you can't enjoy the other things that you have. We all need to take the very best care of ourselves so that we can do the things we love.

> ⑦
> Realise there is always somebody else in the world who's not coping as well as you are.

We all get angry, upset and sad. Everybody feels down when they're having a tough time. Remember there are probably people in the world in worse situations than you.

> ⑧
> Always have fun!

It is very, very important to try to enjoy everything you do. Finding the fun in life means that you and whoever you are with will always be laughing, giggling and smiling, and having a nice time.

> ⑨
> Know that there is time
> in life for everything.

Try really hard never to be in a rush. Slow right down. Even though I ran races on the track all the time, *life* isn't meant to be a race. If you believe that life is too short, then one day soon you will be old – instead, live every moment to its fullest and just be patient. Know that there is a time for everything. You just wait and see!

> ⑩
> Don't be afraid to
> let your imagination
> run wild.

You can be anyone, see anything, do anything! Your imagination can be so much fun, and using it is so easy. Remember that from little things, big things grow.

Cathy Freeman Timeline

1961	My parents had their first child — Gavin Freeman
1966	My big sister, Anne-Marie, was born
1973	I was born!
1974	Norman Freeman was born
1975	Garth Freeman was born
1982	Mum and Bruce got married in Mackay
1983	We moved to Hughenden in North West Queensland (I was ten)
1984	We moved to Moura in central Queensland
1985	We moved (again!) to Coppabella in central Queensland.
1985	We moved back to Mackay (I was twelve)
1987	I went to boarding school at Fairholme College

1990 I competed in my first Commonwealth Games in Auckland, New Zealand. I was sixteen years old and I won my first gold medal in the 100m relay race.

1991 I was awarded Young Australian of the Year

1992 I competed in my first Olympic Games in Barcelona. I missed out on a place in the 400m final, and our team came seventh in the 400m relay race.

1994 My second Commonwealth Games in Victoria, Canada. I won two gold medals for the 400m and the 200m.

1996 I competed in the Olympic Games in Atlanta, USA. I won a silver medal in the 400m behind Marie-José Pérec.

1998 I was awarded Australian of the Year

2000 The year my dream came true! I won a gold medal at the Sydney Olympic Games for my favourite event — the 400m.

2003 I retired from competitive running.

After 2003 I'm looking forward to the next big adventure!

Note on Stolen Generation

If you'd like to read more on the stolen generation (people like Cathy's nanna who were taken away from their parents), check out the following websites:

* http://www.dreamtime.net.au/indigenous/family.cfm
* en.wikipedia.org/wiki/Stolen_Generation

You could also borrow books about it from the library, or ask your teacher about it at school.

Acknowledgements

Creating **Born to Run** was an absolute joy and would not have been possible without the tremendous Penguin team. A special mention must go to Tegan Morrison — your encouragement and guidance was just fantastic! My appreciation must also go to Jane Godwin, Laura Harris, Elissa Christian, Deb Brash, Susie Gibson and Bob Sessions. Thank you.

I acknowledge IMG for recognising the amazing power of books.

To my family and friends, and my darling — thank you for your love!

Last but not least, to all book lovers out there, I hope you enjoy reading **Born to Run** as much as I enjoyed bringing it to you.

Photo Credits

Unless otherwise credited, photographs are from the author's private collection. While evey attempt has been made to contact copyright owners, the publishers would be happy to hear of any omissions so that we can correct these in future editions.

Prelims

p. iii   Scott Barbour/Allsport

Chapter Openers

p. 1   Newspix

p. 12   Both Newspix

p. 62   Newspix

p. 63   Newspix

p. 72   Sport the Library

p. 73   Tony Duffy/Getty Images

p. 80   Sport the Library

p. 81   Sport the Library

p. 88   Newspix

p. 89   Sport the Library

p. 98   Jamie Squire/Allsport

p. 99 Clive Brunskill/Allsport
p. 109 Craig Borrow/Newspix
p. 122 Ray Strange/Newspix
p. 123 David Caird/Newspix

Pictorial Sections
p.   2 Both Newspix
p.   4 *Top*: Newspix; *Bottom Right*: Newspix
p. 6-7 *Bottom*: Newspix
p. 8-9 *Top Right*: Sport the Library
p. 10 Anthony Weate/Newspix
p. 11 Sport the Library
p. 13 Nick Wilson/Newspix
p. 14 Sport the Library
p. 15 Wayne Ludbey/Newspix
p. 16 Craig Borrow/Newspix
p. 17 Patrick Hamilton/Newspix
p. 18 Patrick Hamilton/Newspix
p. 19 Anthony Weate/Newspix
p. 20 Jamie Squire/Allsport
p. 21 *Top*: Kazuhiro Nogi/AFP/Getty Images
       Bottom: Anthony Weate/Newspix
p. 22 Anthony Weate/Newspix

p. 23   Darren England/Allsport
p. 24   Tony Feder/Allsport
p. 25   *Top*: Jeff Darminan/Newspix
        Bottom: Nick Wilson/Allsport
p. 26   Stu Forster/Getty
p. 27   Craig Borrow/Newspix

Do you have a dream to be a champion, too? It might be in soccer, netball, drama, art or gymnastics. If you would like to make your own certificate, just like Cathy did when she was growing up, go to the following website:

www.puffin.com.au/borntorun

All you have to do is type your dream in the blank space (for example, I AM THE WORLD'S GREATEST SOCCER PLAYER or I AM THE WORLD'S GREATEST ARTIST), then print it out and stick it on your bedroom wall or the fridge. That way, you'll be able see it every day!

COME EXPLORING AT

www.penguin.com.au

AND

www.puffin.com.au

FOR

Author and illustrator profiles

Book extracts

Reviews

Competitions

Activities, games and puzzles

Advice for budding authors

Tips for parents

Teacher resources